# Advance Praise for *The Master Coach*

"I have had the great honor of coaching hundreds of executives and managers over the past three decades; I've graduated from four different coaching programs and have read every coaching book I could get my hands on. This book is different. Gregg does a superb job, not only of describing the practices of THE MASTER COACH but also of presenting a compelling case that those who want to really have an impact in their coaching need to bring their entire selves into the coaching relationship and the coaching conversation. This is the best book on coaching that I have read in a long time. It is a must-read for all leaders and non-leaders who aspire to help others make significant changes in their work, careers and, yes . . . their lives."

**Bob Johnson**
Founder, LeaderSearch Executive Coaching Group

"THE MASTER COACH will cause you to PAUSE and REFLECT. It will test your courage through penetrating self-discovery questions that guide you to examine your character and how others see, trust, and connect with you. It will challenge you to coach and lead at a much deeper level, leveraging intense, attitude-changing conversations. It is a coaching model that is essential in helping others realize their full potential."

**Trish Wetzel**
VP, Commercial Operations, Celgene Corporation

"I remember that Gregg wrote an article a few years back called 'Earning the Right to Coach.' That article helped me to become more clear about what I do as a coach and what I needed to do better. And he's been my coach along this journey for the past twenty-five years or so. Gregg writes, 'If I've done my job, you'll feel both challenged and appreciated, encouraged and provoked.' He does all of this and more in this book. He offers, 'If you want to be of significant service to others, become a better coach.' That's absolutely true. As you read it keep one hand open wide—see if you can catch the beautiful gems in this book for yourself."

**Dede Henley**
CEO, The Henley Leadership Group
Author of *The Secret of Sovereignty*

"I have spent the last few years coaching and teaching thousands of organizational leaders how to be more coach-like in their conversations. Leaders who are most effective at coaching realize coaching requires their full presence, character, and attention in every conversation. Many of the coaching books I have read focus on prescribed checklists, but Gregg Thompson's THE MASTER COACH provides insights into the true mastery of coaching. Using insightful stories and compelling yet simple concepts, this book is my new top reading recommendation for my clients. Reading this book has renewed my belief in the power of coaching to improve performance, create positive work environments and build bonds of trust between leaders and their colleagues. But more importantly, its insights compel me to believe that coach-like skills do not stop at the door of the organization. Taking a coach-like approach in all our conversations creates possibilities of better relationships with communities, families and, dare I say, with yourself."

**Jim Boneau**
Principle Leadership Coach & Master Facilitator
The Rumble Group

"Deceptively simple and refreshingly easy to read, THE MASTER COACH is packed with wisdom. I have put this book at the top of the book list for my internal coaches at every level."

**Joanne Vranos**
Head of Human Resources, GasLog Ltd.

"In THE MASTER COACH, Gregg shares the reasons, roles, responsibilities, and results of being a coach. After exploring the vital areas of building trust, values, and communication that are succinctly presented in this very readable book, you will be well-equipped to make a significant difference in the lives of others and you will have the tools to do it."

**Garry Ridge**
President & CEO, WD-40 Company
Coauthor of *Helping People Win at Work*

"Effective coaching is a critical competency of organizational leadership that promotes creativity, elevates performance and resilience, and fosters professional development. These attributes are essential to provide any organization with the competitive advantage it needs to succeed in an environment of continuous change. THE MASTER COACH is an inspiring and brilliantly written guide for success that helps leaders understand the importance of leading with character, building connections, and engaging in extraordinary conversations. THE MASTER COACH should be considered a must-read for every physician leader and healthcare executive who wants to make a real difference."

**James R. Hebl**
Regional Vice-President, Mayo Clinic Health System

"THE MASTER COACH explores authenticity, vulnerability, generosity, integrity, and courage—the hallmarks of great coaches who seek to elevate these same characteristics in those we are privileged to work with. An essential read for anyone looking to bring their highest and best selves to the coaching craft."

**Terry Hogan**
Global Head of Diversity and Director, Talent Management
Co-author of *What is Global Leadership?*
Head of Human Resources, GasLog Ltd.

"I have many good books in my library, but only a small number of truly great ones that I return to time and time again for practical wisdom. THE MASTER COACH has been added to that collection. I have personal experience with Gregg's Character, Connection, and Conversations; this book is simply and extension of who he is. Studied with the proper motivation, it will not only change what you do as a leader . . . it has the potential to transform the ways that you think and interact with those around you. Its goal is to help you build a culture where leaders at all levels are more thoughtful, capable, and effective as they direct, advise, teach, mentor and coach others.  If you want to take your current skills and organization to the next level, this book offers a great ROI."

**Tom Steipp**
Former CEO, Symmetricom, Liquidmetal Technologies

"Having had the opportunity to lead and serve patients as a general thoracic surgeon, colleagues as the CEO of the Mayo Clinic Arizona, and now students as the Director of the School for the Science of Health Care Delivery at ASU, I truly believe in the importance of servant leadership in achieving great results. The essence of this model is the ability to coach your team members to grow and attain their most ambitious goals. In my experience, Gregg Thompson exemplifies a "master coach" and has the great ability to teach others through word and action to be the best coaches they can be. Improved leadership by understanding the importance of coaching leads ultimately to improved patient care. I highly recommend THE MASTER COACH as a critical read for all leaders in health care."

**Dr. Victor Trastek**
Former CEO, Mayo Clinic Arizona
Director, School for the Science of Health Care Delivery, ASU

"In a refreshing, direct, and very personal voice, Gregg Thompson offers deep insights and learning about the long but very rewarding path to becoming a master coach. With its structured and clear approach, THE MASTER COACH served me extremely well in fine tuning my coaching perspective, both as a professional coach and as a leader in the corporate environment. The book is a joy to read and provides profound inspiration!"

**Peter Rauber**
Senior Director of Engineering
Qualcomm

# The
# Master
# Coach

# The
# Master
# Coach

---

*Leading with Character,*
*Building Connections, and Engaging in*
*Extraordinary Conversations*

---

## GREGG THOMPSON

SelectBooks, Inc.
*New York*

This edition published by SelectBooks, Inc.
For information address SelectBooks, Inc., New York, New York.

First Edition

ISBN 978-1-59079-419-7

Library of Congress Cataloging-in-Publication Data

Names: Thompson, Gregg, 1950- author.
Title: The master coach : leading with character, building connections, and
  engaging in extraordinary conversations / Gregg Thompson.
Description: First Edition. | New York : SelectBooks, 2017. | Series:
  Bluepoint leadership series | Includes index.
Identifiers: LCCN 2016053164 | ISBN 9781590794197 (hardback)
Subjects: LCSH: Employees--Coaching of. | Executive ability.
Classification: LCC HF5549.5.C53 T4598 2017 | DDC 658.3/124--dc23 LC record
available at https://lccn.loc.gov/2016053164

Book design by Janice Benight

Manufactured in the United States of America
10 9 8 7 6 5 4 3 2

*This book is dedicated to three precious souls—*
*Jordyn, Elliott, and Violet—*
*who have taught me the power of innocence, serendipity,*
*and patience in coaching.*

# Contents

# Foreword

Every day, opportunities for entrepreneurship, innovation, and execution excellence stare us in the face, especially in a global environment that's moving into greater complexity and at rapidly increasing speeds. My job at GE is to equip our strategic customers to seize these opportunities by generating exceptional performance in their teams and organizations. I am tasked with both developing a new generation of leaders and helping retool seasoned leaders so that they can pivot and capitalize on the many prospects the new marketplace is presenting. In this endeavor, coaching is one of the most powerful tools available—and one that our customers are requesting with growing frequency.

Unfortunately, the idea of coaching is misunderstood by too many leaders and still perceived as a last-resort fix to deal with substandard performance and dysfunctional behaviors. When Gregg Thompson gave me the manuscript for *The Master Coach*, I was delighted to finally have in my hands a book that sets the record straight. Gregg makes a compelling case that coaching is not just a set of predetermined interpersonal practices but rather, a sincere willingness to make a significant (and sometimes deep) personal investment in others. Of course, there are good coaching practices that every leader should learn. But I believe, as does Gregg, that *who you are* in a coaching conversation is often more important than what you say or do.

Building on this core principle, Gregg has not written a conventional book on coaching practices, though it is an exceptionally practical guide. He has written a true invitation to mastery. As you read, you will be inspired to *become* a coach—to earn the right to guide others in their development. There is a thread of positive tension that is drawn from the first page to the last. This tension is a challenge to mediocrity; both in leaders and in those they lead.

Refreshingly, this book tells the truth about coaching. It is not all hearts and rainbows. Because it is such a personal endeavor, coaching can be a perilous undertaking, requiring enormous commitment and courage. But I believe that it is worth it and, if mastered, can provide you a lasting competitive advantage as an authentic leader who produces exceptional outcomes. When you truly master the art of coaching, you will have the ability to make, as Gregg asserts, "an indelible mark on the work, careers, and lives of those you coach." In the end, this book is really about getting more out of your work by putting more of yourself into it. Putting more of yourself into your work, in a deliberate and caring way, provides a critical component to the attainment of mastery.

**Robert T. Cancalosi**
Director of Customer Leadership Education, GE Crotonville

# Preface

If you have chosen to read this book, you have high aspirations, and I applaud you for that. You were drawn to the promise of mastery. You might not have considered, before looking at this book cover, that being a "master coach" was possible for you. I'm guessing you already have some experience in guiding or leading others, and perhaps you want to improve your skills, or pick up some helpful techniques. As you turn these pages, you may find yourself engaging with a potential that could lift you much higher than you set out to climb. That's what great coaching does. It awakens people to possibilities they have not yet recognized, and helps them achieve their own version of mastery.

As a reader of books on coaching, it's likely that you fall into one of two categories. You may be a businessperson—a leader or manager—who recognizes that coaching is something you need to be doing with your team, or introducing throughout your organization. Perhaps you are being asked to abandon traditional performance management and embrace a more coach-like orientation in your day-to-day work. I am blessed with the opportunity to work with wonderful people like you every day. I know how important you are, no matter where in the organization you serve, and how much more effective you can become by supervising less, stressing less, checking up less, and coaching more. The ideas in this book have been designed to help you become a Leader Coach—someone who is able to bring the art of coaching into your everyday leadership activity. (In this book I use the term "Leader Coach" interchangeably with the terms "coach" and "master coach," since so many of those to whom I am speaking fall into this category.)

As a Leader Coach, you can have a profound impact on those with whom you work and encourage each of them to do the same to others. The perspectives and skills I will be sharing in this book are as relevant on the factory floor as they are in the boardroom. I hope that you will find in these pages the confidence, inspiration, and tools to make coaching part of the core connective tissue of your company.

Alternately, you may be a consultant, life coach, or executive coach looking to raise your game and have a greater impact. As an executive leadership coach myself, I know the challenges, rewards, and possibilities that you navigate every day. I wrote this book to help you become the kind of coach who brings extraordinary value to leaders and is remembered with gratitude and respect. This book may teach you new skills and approaches, but it may also simply highlight some of the things you are already doing and help you make them more conscious and deliberate. I hope that it may challenge you to shift the way you serve others and help shape the next chapter of your life and career. As you develop mastery in your own coaching work, I hope you will also pass on the perspective and power of coaching to each and every leader with whom you work, so that it can spread to every level of your organization, even those you never directly touch.

The term "coach" is both a verb and a noun, but in this book you will find that the emphasis is on the latter. In other words, my primary intent is to share with you what it means to *be* a coach, rather than simply teaching you coaching techniques. That doesn't mean you won't find practical, step-by-step advice in these pages; you will. But you'll find something else that is far more important and valuable if you aspire to be not just a good coach but a master coach. You'll be introduced to the traits, values, perspectives, and attitudes that distinguish those coaches who are always remembered with profound gratitude from those who are quickly forgotten.

I have personally coached hundreds of people, and Bluepoint Leadership Development, the extraordinary company I am honored to lead, has trained over ten thousand leaders, managers, and individual contributors to bring coaching into their organizations. This has given me a unique vantage point from which to observe patterns and commonalities among those who are successful in the field. That's not to say there's a simple formula for turning an average coach into a great coach. Coaching is a human communication and change process that is as individual as we are. Yes, you can adopt best practices and learn from those with greater experience than you, but who you will be as a coach cannot be separated from who you are as a human being. That is what gives coaching such potency; it is also what makes it a demanding path to walk.

Becoming a master coach is an internal affair. While this book is replete with timeless concepts and proven coaching approaches, you will not find a predetermined set of interpersonal steps that you can memorize and employ to do great coaching. If you are looking for such steps, you will be disappointed. I believe that it is far more important for me to help you develop "the coach within" so that you will be well equipped to determine your own best steps in every conversation.

As you read this book, I hope you will be drawn into an inner dialogue between the ideas on the page and your own values, aspirations, and goals. It may be uncomfortable at some times, exciting at others. If I've done my job, you'll feel both challenged and appreciated, encouraged and provoked. A word of caution: the coaching process requires commitment, investment, and action from you and from those you coach. Wishing will make it so only happens in the movies. In my experience, wishing is where the process of dreaming stops for far too many people. I have written this book to equip you to help people change the aspects of their lives that have real impact: their behavior, their work, their relationships, and their attitude. These are the changes that people need to make to turn dreams into reality.

That being said, it is important to note that I believe in the power of optimism and positivity. In fact, this book is heavily influenced by the principle of appreciative inquiry (seeking the very best in others) and positive psychology (creating meaning, fulfillment, and happiness). Coaching someone to keep their dreams in their mind as often as possible is easy; confronting them with their responsibility for their unmet aspirations and challenging them to take control of their own future is much harder. I am inviting you to take this road less travelled.

This book will introduce you to the key principles that are the foundations of my approach to coaching. These are not solely my ideas, but draw on the universal tenets of human nature and human interaction that have served people since the dawn of civilization, as well as cutting-edge insights from business, psychology, and neuroscience. I hope that the book will make these profound ideas and principles accessible and relevant. Building on this foundation, it will guide you through the three core dimensions of coaching mastery: Character, Connection, and Conversation. In the chapters on Character, we will engage with the all-important question, have you earned the right to coach? We will examine the values, characteristics, and behaviors that will encourage others to welcome you to be a catalyst for their personal development. In the chapters on Connection, we will focus on what it takes to establish and maintain the unique relationship necessary for coaching. And in the chapters on Conversation, we will explore the pathways and practices that make every dialogue with a master coach so enriching and potentially transformative.

For the past twenty-five years I have coached and been coached by some incredibly talented people. I consider it a rare privilege and profound honor to work at such a deep personal level with each and every one of them. About ten years ago, I wrote the book *Unleashed!* with the assistance of Susanne Biro. Since then, I have designed several workshops and, together with my colleagues at Bluepoint, provided coach training to thousands of organization leaders every year. We have learned much from these workshops, and while *The Master Coach* draws on many of the same universal principles as *Unleashed!*, I have incorporated a decade's worth of learning to create a book that is a much more comprehensive and personal guide to mastering the art of coaching. This book represents the sum of my own learning thus far, and I owe a debt of gratitude to every person who has contributed to it.

I would be honored to act as your coach for the time it takes you to journey through this book. Mastery is clearly within your reach.

# Acknowledgments

Throughout my career, I have been profoundly influenced by three remarkable teachers in the fields of Organization Development and human potential: Carl Rogers, Herb Sheppard, and Bob Tannenbaum. Every word in this book is rooted in their pioneering ideas about how people learn, change, and interact. It is my most fervent hope that this book honors their work in some small way.

Joan Peterson, Bill Gardner, Peter Rauber, Patricia Wetzel, Ingvild Saether, Bob Johnson, Lynn Harrison, and Jason Thompson gave generously of their time to read an early manuscript and provide invaluable comments that resulted in a much more readable book. Many, many thanks.

I am greatly indebted to Bryn Meredith, COO of Bluepoint Leadership Development, whose masterful management of the company has provided me the resources and allowed me the freedom to write this book. Thank you, Bryn.

Great coaches challenge us to move from intention to action and hold us accountable to do just that. An unexpected coaching session with Steve Erickson of New York Life during a leadership development workshop moved this book from being an oft-talked-about wish to a roughly crafted first draft. Steve, if not for you, I might be still spinning castles in the air.

Many thanks go to Ashley Lee and Jon Thompson for their untiring creative work in producing the cover design, and to Kenzi Sugihara and Kenichi Sugihara of SelectBooks for shepherding this book all the way to the bookshelves.

I have been blessed with an extraordinary executive assistant, Nancy Tansy, who does an amazing job of editing my writing and correcting my grammar. Always there and always appreciated, Nancy.

Ellen Daly has been much more than the lead editor on this project. She has been a brilliant writing partner and is largely responsible for the best parts of the book. It is no overstatement when I assert that, without her, the book would not have been written.

# Introduction

For the past few decades I have been an executive coach, hired by organizations to help their senior leaders with the difficult task of making significant changes in their behavior. What Gregg Thompson understands is that coaching need not be reserved for a company's top executives; nor is it the exclusive domain of professional coaches like me. As businesses become more complex and dynamic, there is an increasing need for managers at every level to provide coaching to their team members. Yet, in all my years of working with organizations, one of the most common complaints I hear from people is that their managers fall short in this regard. Teaching managers effective coaching skills is one of the best investments an organization can make, and I know of no one more qualified to impart this knowledge than Gregg. In *The Master Coach*, he distills his learning and insights gained from providing coach training to thousands of leaders into a compelling and engaging book that is relevant to all of us.

When done well, coaching is one of the most effective human resource development processes available. But as Gregg points out in this profound yet practical book, to *do* great coaching work, one must authentically *be* a coach. Coaching, he writes, is "a complex human-to-human relationship whose ultimate success depends much more on the character and intention of the coach than on any particular method he or she uses." With this in mind, he dedicates a large part of this book to illuminating the character traits, perspectives, attitudes, values, and behaviors that distinguish great coaches. Focusing on topics like integrity, authenticity, and trustworthiness, he inspires and challenges readers to "earn the right to coach."

With Character established as the foundational element of great coaching, Gregg adds two more: Connection and Conversation. Here, he showcases the repertoire of coaching insights, skills, and tools that he has developed and implemented in companies like American Airlines, New York Life, Celgene, American Express, and many more. Drawing on the wealth of experience that has made his programs the choice of numerous Fortune 100 companies, *The Master Coach* could well become the definitive book on creating a coaching culture.

There are many good coaching systems out there. But the difference between a good coach and a Master Coach comes down to the essential message of this book: coaching is not merely about what the coach says or does; it is about who he or she is. Readers who take his message to heart and put it into practice will find that mastery is indeed within their reach. Gregg's penetrating insights into the coaching mindset make The Master Coach essential reading for any leader who is serious about unleashing the human potential of their workforce.

Life is good.

**Marshall Goldsmith**
*Thinkers 50* #1 Leadership Thinker and
#1 Executive Coach in the World
#1 *New York Times* best-selling author of *Triggers, MOJO,*
and *What Got You Here Won't Get You There*

# PART I

# Foundations of Coaching

# 1

# On Becoming a Master Coach

*The time that leads to mastery is dependent on the intensity of our focus.*

—ROBERT GREENE, *Mastery*

For some, being a leader today is a wonderful, rewarding adventure. For others, it is a thankless, underappreciated chore. This has probably always been the case. But the world is changing, and the very notion of what a leader is, and what a leader does, is changing with it. First, the idea of having a hero-leader perched at the top of the organization is rapidly fading. Effective leadership is now needed and expected at all levels of the organization. Second, positional power is waning. It matters less that you have the title of Manager, Director, or Vice-President and more that others see you as a person of purpose, influence, and inspiration. And third, organizations are becoming much more nebulous and disorderly. They are often spread over vast geographical distances and interconnected with multiple other companies. Technology continues to disrupt every industry at shorter and shorter intervals. And while leaders struggle to compete in this fast-paced global marketplace, they also face increasing expectations for their businesses to have a positive social and environmental impact, moving into territory once reserved for NGOs and governments. Demands for transparency and integrity are higher than ever, and a single social-media-empowered customer can do damage that would have been unimaginable in any other era.

In response to this daunting set of challenges, much creative thinking has been done about how we might re-envision the workplace, restructure organizations, and reinvent traditional management hierarchies. Some even go so far as to reimagine capitalism itself. But as management expert Gary Hamel astutely observes, "the pay-off from reforming capitalism, while substantial, pales in comparison to the gains that could be reaped from creating organizations that are as fully capable as the people who work within them."[1]

Organizations are populated by individuals—unique men and women with all their talents, capacities, and strengths as well as their idiosyncrasies, moods, and flaws. These are the things that add vitality and richness to organizational life. New generations of employees, or associates, as they are now often called, are less content than ever to be treated like cogs in a machine or even "human resources." They want to be respected and valued as people. They want to learn and develop. They want to contribute and be part of something special.

As traditional command-and-control pyramids give way to distributed-authority networks, organizations are flattening out. And millennials, who will make up more than 75 percent of the workforce by 2025, care about doing meaningful work—so much so that more than 50 percent say they would take a pay cut to find a job that matches their values.[2] Organizations that are moving into the future will bear more resemblance to purpose-driven communities than profit-driven hierarchies. Business is becoming more collaborative, more complex, and more chaotic.

In the midst of this turmoil, doubling down on a highly directive style of management simply doesn't work. But what should leaders and managers do instead? Often these are people who have been hired for their industry expertise, their innovative thinking, their business acumen, their technical know-how, their strategic vision, or their role-specific skill set. They likely have solid interpersonal skills and are confident managing teams—keeping them productive, focused, and organized. But this authority-centered management is an approach that works for processes, systems, numbers, or logistics. It's just not particularly effective for getting the best out of people. As Hamel puts it, "Initiative, imagination and passion can't be commanded—they're gifts. Every day, employees choose whether to bring those gifts to work or not, and the evidence suggests they usually leave them at home."[3]

One such piece of evidence is the depressing data on "employee engagement." Gallup's latest global survey showed that as few as 13 percent of employees described themselves as truly engaged in their work.[4] That means that an incalculable amount of human talent, energy, intelligence, and innovation is being lost every day in almost every workplace. And it points to what I see as the core challenge and opportunity facing today's leaders: fully engaging their teams and unleashing the creative potential of the men and women who show up to work every day.

Look around your workplace right now—at its cubicles and its hallways, its meeting rooms or labs, its factory floor or its showroom. Any place where people come to work, you will find enormous, untapped potential waiting to be developed and deployed. If companies can find a way to truly unleash the full capacities of the human beings within them, they won't have to worry so much about reinventing their workplaces. Their people will do that for them. And when it comes to unleashing human potential, there is one process that has consistently proven to be more effective than any other: coaching.

## THE LEADER AS COACH

When I was growing up, coaches were the guys with the loud voices and even louder whistles out on the sports field. But these days, coaching is everywhere. From the basketball court to the boardroom, it is recognized as a critical element in the pursuit of excellence. We have life coaches, parenting coaches, relationship coaches, wealth coaches, health coaches—the list goes on. And within the business world, coaching has soared in popularity, becoming the fastest growing human resource development process today.

Everyone may be using the term, but we don't necessarily all mean the same thing. In business, coaching can refer to anything from tracking performance to advising on career development. Unfortunately, most contemporary approaches to coaching are essentially some combination of problem-solving and action-planning processes. True coaching, is something much more rare. It is a co-creative, co-learning process that demands more than the basic communication and interpersonal practices that most leaders have mastered. Here's the definition I like: *Coaching is a powerful interpersonal process that stimulates and equips a person to perform at a higher level while accelerating their development.*

Two words are key here: performance and development. Ultimately, the test of any coach's success is whether there are visibly higher performance and accelerated development in those being coached. But there is a profound twist. As discussed throughout this book, when you are at your best as a coach, the person being coached receives all the credit for this progress. If you are seeking immediate recognition, honors, and adulation, coaching is likely not for you. If, on the other hand, you simply want to be of significant service to others, it likely is. Coaching is a process that has the sole purpose of unleashing the potential of the individual being coached. As you become a good coach, a great coach, a *master* coach, you will make an indelible mark on the work, careers, and lives of those you coach. A master coach is a catalyst for sustained personal change in individuals that in turn will tangibly impact the organizations in which they work and communities in which they live.

Nothing compares to coaching when it comes to helping people perform at their best and accelerate their careers. Not re-engineering, not team building, not quality improvement programs. Coaching works because it is focused on the individual rather than on the organization and its processes. Even mediocre coaching can produce remarkable results. Individuals become energized (or re-energized) about their work, take full ownership of their performance and their careers, find and rejuvenate long-lost talents, and make major shifts in their contribution levels. Go and speak to anyone in your organization who has significantly increased their performance and you will find a coach involved somewhere, even if that is not their official title.

While we're defining terms, there's another that needs to be mentioned. A coach has no purpose without someone to coach. I use the term "Talent" to describe the person receiving coaching, in recognition of the natural abilities and potential that he or she possesses. I'll say more about the thinking behind this term in chapter three, but for now, the Talent refers to the individual who is receiving coaching. It is important to note that the Talent can be anyone with whom you are interacting: your team members, your colleagues, your manager, even your customer.

As a leader, manager, or team member, you are perfectly positioned to become a master coach. This is not a role reserved for psychologists or professional executive coaches. In fact, I believe it is increasingly recognized as an essential competency at every organizational level, as the traditional functions of leadership are being distributed more and more broadly. There's no way that a single heroic leader can drive all the complexity of decision-making and execution from the top down. If a company is to be agile, responsive, and able to keep pace with its fast-changing environment, people at every level need to have the tools, the confidence, and the will to be leaders in their own teams and throughout the organization.

Leadership becomes everyone's business. And the type of leadership required is the ability to influence the people you directly touch and interact with every day. Training managers to coach is the most effective means of making them into good line-of-sight leaders. Coaching needs to happen throughout an organization and become an integrated part of how managers work with their teams and their colleagues.

Everywhere I go, from Boston to Bangkok, senior leaders are recognizing that creating a coaching culture is the key to unlocking the talent that's hiding in plain sight in their workplaces. In fact, a 2015 study by the International Coaching Federation (ICF) and the Human Capital Institute (HCI) found that 81 percent of organizations surveyed planned to expand their scope of managers/leaders using coaching skills.[5] I'm encouraged by these statistics, but I also know that despite its growing popularity, certain misconceptions about coaching are pervasive. If the promise of a coaching culture is to be truly fulfilled, greater clarity needs to be brought to the critical difference between picking up a few coaching skills and becoming a master coach.

## COACHING IS A WAY OF BEING

If there is one message you take away from this book, let it be this: *Coaching is a way of being, not doing.* Despite what many authors will have you believe, there is no universal formula for coaching—it's far too big an endeavor to be compressed into a finite number of steps. It is not a nice, neat cognitive process involving the exchange of feedback, insights, and action plans. To be honest, it might better be described as a muddled, awkward expedition full of chaos, experimentation, self-learning, disappointment, and elation. It is a complex human-to-human relationship whose ultimate success depends much more on the character and intention of the coach than on any particular method he or she uses.

That said, coaching can be learned. But you must be prepared to learn by changing, to *become* a coach rather than adopt a set of skills. This book will guide you in that developmental journey. It will also provide you with proven tools, techniques, and approaches, but these will always be secondary to the transformation of the person who is using them. My purpose is not to introduce you to one specific coaching technique but rather to introduce you to the coach inside of you, and to help that coach become a master. My hope is that if I am successful, while you may not always be engaging in a conversation, you will always be a coach. Coaching is an attitude and a commitment to having a positive influence on the lives of others. When we master this art, it is not something we turn off and on at will; it is a way of being.

Because of the personal nature of the journey, becoming a master coach is not easy. And it is not a path that comes to an end, with a certification to mark your achievement. Master coaches are always learning and growing because they know their ability to coach is inseparable from their own development. But it is one of the best investments of time and energy you could possibly make if you want to have a real impact on others and become a better person with a richer life in the process.

## YOU ARE SUFFICIENT

A coach is something you become, but it is also simply something you are. The path to mastery in the arena of coaching is sometimes counterintuitive, because this is one of the few areas of life in which accumulating greater knowledge won't necessarily make you more proficient. Rather, it is a journey of going deeper into yourself, stripping away obstacles and limiting beliefs, and becoming more confident in who you truly are.

Have you ever come across a great book, a website, or an inspiring video and immediately said to yourself, "My sister/ brother/friend/boss/child needs to read/see this"? We dutifully pass along references and links in hopes that the pearls of wisdom contained within will change the recipient's life. Look at the seemingly endless quotations, sayings, and poems that one can find on almost any Facebook page. Sadly, too many coaches, even professional coaches, do the same thing, hoping it will enhance their coaching. It doesn't. Don't do it. This well-intentioned but counterproductive practice is the antithesis of great coaching because it sends out the erroneous message that the answer is out there, somewhere, in something someone else has written or said. It isn't—no matter how brilliant, insightful, or relevant their words may be. The answer is in the coaching process. It just needs to be found.

As a coach, remember these three powerful words: *You are sufficient.* You do not need books and videos or anything else to back you up. Trust the process. Trust yourself. And most of all, trust the Talent. *You are sufficient.* Those three words sum up the essence of what every master coach knows. All you need to bring into the coaching process is you. The answers will be found right there, in the moment, not in any external resources you may bring to the table during or after the session.

I know this is a challenging message to hear. In a world that teaches us to revere experts, it is scary to put them aside. When we have built our careers on knowledge, credentials, and tools, it is an act of courage to put these on hold and simply be ourselves. And it is even more courageous to do so while acknowledging that we don't have the answers—the Talent does. To trust the process that much can be profoundly disconcerting, but it's the essence of great coaching.

The core thesis of this approach is that the pathway forward is always best discovered within the conversation between the coach and the Talent. That's not to say books, resources, knowledge, and expertise aren't helpful, but they are secondary. They especially should never be used to dampen the uncomfortable ambiguity and uncertainty that opens up when you start to explore the uncharted waters of human performance and potential.

## WHAT A COACH IS . . .
## AND WHAT A COACH IS NOT

It's likely that, without giving it a name, you have been the recipient of great coaching at some point in your life. Consider for a moment the people who have influenced you most and helped you become the person you are today. Were they people who merely imparted information or those who taught you a skill set or inspired by example? When I ask this question, what I usually hear is that some of the most impactful people in our lives are those who believe in us, see possibilities we can't see, encourage us to go further than we would do alone, and challenge us to transcend limitations. They are people who listen, who truly care about our success, and who invest in us those rarest of commodities: time and attention. They remind us of what is most important to us and encourage us to be the best versions of ourselves. Those people are our coaches, whether we call them by that name or not.

I have been blessed with many such people in my life. I remember one day when I was walking through the plant with Arnie, a colleague of mine on a small engineering team. We had a coworker who was a real pain. He was obstinate, opinionated, and miserable most of the time. I knew that he annoyed Arnie as much as me, so I made a comment about him. "Yes, Gregg, you are right," Arnie replied. "John is a hard man to love but he is worth it." I was struck to the core by these few words. I was embarrassed. Arnie had not criticized me directly; he just reminded me of my own values. He was being a coach in that moment, though he probably did not know it. Specifically, he brought to mind a commitment I had made, early in life, to be like my father, who I adored and respected immensely. He made a point of never speaking poorly about others behind their backs. He would not even listen to such a conversation. I had just violated my commitment to emulate him and I felt it intensely. It was a pivotal moment in my own development when I reaffirmed the centrality of that value in my life. And it would not have happened without Arnie.

Coaching draws on and overlaps many other disciplines, synthesizing some of the best that has been learned about human development and potential. But it distinguishes itself in important ways from other kinds of developmental relationships we may have, in business or in life. Because the term is often loosely used for many kinds of engagement, it's critical to take a moment and look at what true coaching is not. If you are in a leadership role, you are likely to take many different roles, at different moments, as circumstances demand. But understanding what coaching is and why it differs from many other roles can help you to take maximum advantage of this powerful and often under-appreciated way of relating.

**A Coach Is Not a Friend.** As a coach you may be friendly, but you are not a friend. A coach is an advocate who wants the best from those he or she is coaching. Your job is to hold the Talent accountable, challenging them to grow and do more than they think they can do. You may push, pull, and stretch them in ways that may feel uncomfortable. My heart goes out to the wonderful people that I coach because I know that engaging in real coaching is an act of significant courage. All key assumptions will be challenged, long-held beliefs will be tested, comforting stories about personal limitations will be exposed. Finally, unlike a friendship, the coaching relationship is unilateral—it is exclusively focused on the talent and his or her goals, not the coach, her family, his golf handicap, or what she did over the weekend.

**A Coach Is Not a Consultant.** Some consultants may be coach-like, but a coach plays a very different role than a consultant. Consultants tend to come in to provide analysis or recommendations for how to fix a gap, solve a problem, or seize an opportunity. This is often critically important for leaders and their companies, but it is diametrically opposed to a coaching approach. As a coach, you move away from gap-analysis and instead look at what works best in the situation and what can be done better. Your focus is on potentials, not problems.

A consultant adds value by investigating, assessing, and then applying their expertise to the situation to come up with a plan and help the leader move forward with that plan. The coach, on the other hand, believes that the solution sits with the Talent. The coach knows that he or she is less equipped to come up with the path forward than the Talent. The unique power of coaching comes from helping others draw upon resources within themselves that have been previously hidden or avoided. Something very powerful, nearly magical, happens when the answer comes from within.

**A Coach Is Not a Therapist or Counselor.** It is important to understand the difference between coaching and counseling, particularly counseling of the therapeutic kind. Since both coaches and counselors utilize essentially the same tools and processes (e.g., trusting relationships, intense dialogue, and penetrating questions) it is easy to see why many blur the line between the two disciplines. However, as a coach your role is not to be the Talent's psychotherapist. Coaching and counseling are both powerful processes that can help to improve lives, but they have fundamentally different approaches. Understanding the difference will help you avoid getting drawn into a role you are unprepared for.

One of my colleagues recently told me that she was coaching a client who persistently spoke about feeling "bummed out" or depressed. Knowing the bounds of her role as a coach, she wisely pushed him to seek professional help from a counselor or psychotherapist. Unfortunately, her client was resistant, and after several tough conversations she was forced to give him an ultimatum: "I can't continue to coach you unless you get some supplemental help." They parted ways for a year, and then the client resumed the coaching relationship, having engaged in counseling and mastered his depression. Coaching is not the antidote for deeply troubled and significantly distressed individuals.

I applauded my colleague for her professional integrity with this client and her commitment to his best interests even if it meant losing his business. Some coaches would not have shown that degree of clarity about where their role begins and ends. Their natural desire to be helpful and see a client through a rough patch can often tempt them into areas in which they are not qualified to help.

Counseling or therapy usually involves digging deep, revisiting past events to help someone heal a psychological wound and, in doing so, find relief from its negative effects on the present. Counseling looks backward, while coaching looks primarily toward the future, seeking clarity of purpose and aspirations that will give life and work greater meaning. Coaching is for people who are looking to make a significant improvement in their work, career, relationships, or life. While this approach may touch on a wide range of topics in pursuit of its goal, it always remains guided by the question, "How can you act or think differently *to create* a better future?"

Although there is a marked difference between the approach of coaches and therapists, we are all working in the area of human potential, aspirations, and relationships, and our work is often complementary.

**A Coach Is Not a Mentor.** It is easy to confuse coaching with mentoring, but these are two distinctly different processes. Mentoring typically takes place between someone with greater experience and knowledge in a field and someone who is newer to that field. As discussed in more depth in chapter two, coaching does not require that the coach have greater experience or knowledge than the Talent. The coach opens the door to an inquiry, a discovery and learning process that unfolds in the moment, whereas the mentor draws on past life experience, wisdom, and lessons learned to guide a typically younger or less experienced colleague.

***A Coach Is Not a Teacher.*** Often, near the end of a coaching relationship, clients will thank me and add, "You taught me so much." But when I differ and press them to identify the specific things I have taught them, thankfully they are usually unable to do so. They have learned much but I have not been their teacher. I am not the holder of knowledge, nor they the receiver. A coach is different from a teacher in many ways, but the key difference is that a classical teacher-student relationship is a one-directional connection in which the teacher imparts information to the student, who learns. A coaching relationship, by contrast, is a learning partnership between the coach and the Talent in which the coach does not teach, but rather learns with the Talent. In partnership, they pursue a process of mutual inquiry and discovery.

To summarize, the key distinction between coaching and other helping roles is focus. Coaching focuses on the achievement of specific Talent-generated goals and the creation of a significant commitment to action and change. Counseling and therapy focus on personal and emotional healing. Consulting and training focus on specific projects, content, and competencies. Mentoring focuses on experience acquisition and career pathing.

## CHARACTER, CONNECTION, CONVERSATION: THE THREE DIMENSIONS OF COACHING

Now that I've talked about the various things coaching is not, let me share with you my model for what it is. Coaching consists of three core dimensions. In keeping with the concepts I've presented so far, none of these are simple formulas or prescriptive steps; rather, they are the foundation stones upon which you will build a coaching practice that is as individual as you are, and those you coach.

***Character*** is the most essential dimension of coaching. Put most simply, character is about *you*—who you are as a human being and the qualities you possess that convince others to trust you. It's not just your individual personality, but the deeper qualities such as integrity, healthy self-esteem, and noble intention. The quality of your character is what earns you the right to coach others.

**Connection** is your relationship with the Talent. All significant change occurs through the medium of your relationship with the person you are coaching. The coaching connection is a peer-to-peer relationship built on mutual trust. At once caring and challenging, dangerous and supportive, this relationship has unique qualities that make it conducive to catalyzing growth and development. It is part of the coach's job to ensure that this relationship is established before coaching can begin.

**Conversation** is the dialogue you have together. The process of successful coaching involves much more than just talking with others about their goals and dreams. The coaching conversation can be risky, in that it often takes both coach and Talent out of their comfort zones. The coaching conversation not only uncovers new ideas and generates innovative solutions; it results in entirely new attitudes and behaviors, and forges commitments to make significant, sustained personal changes.

## The 3C Model of Coaching

A large part of this book is dedicated to discussing these core elements in detail. As a leader, you will be encouraged to reflect on three big questions: Have I earned the right to coach? Do I establish the kinds of relationships necessary for coaching? Am I willing to engage in the intensely honest conversations that stimulate profound learning, development, and change? To be candid, we all fall short to some degree when measured by our honest responses to these questions. The Master Coach, however, courageously confronts these questions and uses them to guide his or her own development.

## THE GREATEST GIFT

Coaching is not a panacea for all our problems in life. I'll be the first to admit it has its limits. It saddens me when I read promotional pieces on coaches' websites that promise to help people "reach unlimited potential" or "realize their most ambitious dreams." As a coach I can only take the talent as far as he or she is willing and ready to go. What I can promise, however, is that as a coach I can help someone see a tomorrow that is better, in some way, than today, and if they want to, they can step into it.

At the risk of sounding too idealistic, there are few things in life that are more rewarding or more meaningful than being instrumental in helping others have better lives. I often refer to coaching as a *calling* or *mission* because I believe there is something inside each of us that comes alive when we have an opportunity to be of real service to others.

This may seem like an overly grandiose term for something you do as part of your job. But if you think about it, our jobs consume most of our waking hours and much of our human energy. As the poet and essayist Annie Dillard writes, "How we spend our days is, of course, how we spend our lives."[6] And anyone who has ever had a miserable job or a terrible boss knows how soul-destroying it can be when the office you go to day after day feels like a dead end. How we feel about our work has a huge impact on how we feel about everything. Sure, helping people be more engaged in their jobs is a key leadership practice but, maybe even more importantly, it is a way of helping them thrive in their lives.

If Leader Coaches can help people blossom at work, enjoy work, look forward to work, we are not just doing leadership work, we are doing life-work. Even if you are coaching someone on a relatively narrow job-related issue, you are helping them use their skills and talents to create a better life for themselves. In its truest form, coaching at work is about helping people learn and grow, bring their very best talents to the tasks at hand, and thrive in the process.

The shift your coaching catalyzes may be a revolutionary one—a breakthrough insight that seems to occur overnight. Or it may be a slow, evolutionary change, a process of gradual adaption over weeks, months, or years. However it happens, when it does, it's unmistakable and is the most powerful gift we can give our organizations: the liberation of human talent, one individual at a time.

# 2

# The Coaching Perspective

*The fact that we live at the bottom of a deep gravity well, on the surface of a gas covered planet going around a nuclear fireball 90 million miles away and think this to be normal is obviously some indication of how skewed our perspective tends to be.*

—DOUGLAS ADAMS, *The Salmon of Doubt*

I was somewhat surprised when Tavish accepted my invitation for coffee. He was known for being very focused on his work. "Intense" and "driven" were probably the words that best captured his reputation. I'd met him when we sat on the same advisory board and had become curious to learn more about him and his organization. A very successful entrepreneur, he has grown his one-person lumber business into a thriving organization employing a few thousand people. After exchanging pleasantries in his small plain office, I asked him if he would share what was unique about his approach to his business and organization.

I expected him to talk about vision, innovation, inspiration, or the like. But he immediately answered, "Faith. Faith in our people, faith in our customers, and faith in myself. Everything that I do as a leader is an expression of faith. To be honest, having true faith in others is often the hardest thing for me, but is probably the most important source of success in our business. To me, it is very simple: the more faith I have in others, the better work they do and the more money we make. It's not complex. It's just hard. It is very easy to let doubt, disbelief, and judgment get in the way."

As Tavish spoke, I understood why I'd been so impressed with him. His philosophy of leadership resonated deeply with my own beliefs about coaching. In fact, if I had to sum up the essence of coaching in one sentence, it would be this: *Coaching is an act of faith in others.*

The master coach sees other people as being full of potential. He or she always makes the assumption that human beings are naturally talented, innately resourceful, and able to learn and change. They are fully capable of making their own decisions and solving their own problems. They can seize their own opportunities. Furthermore, the wise coach knows that when people make their own decisions, create their own solutions, and solve their own problems, they are much more committed to the resulting actions. Coaches see others as reservoirs of untapped abilities, many of which may be unknown even to the person who possesses them, and they see themselves as catalysts who may help reveal and realize these unseen possibilities.

What I've just described is what I call the coaching perspective. A perspective is a window on the world, a particular way of seeing and relating to other people. Foundational to all good coaching is a shift in perspective. Without authentically adopting a coaching perspective, no amount of skillful conversations or interpersonal processes will make you an effective coach.

Everything that a coach says and does is predicated on who the coach *is* and how the coach *sees*. No one is truly objective—we look out at the world around us through the complex filters of our own beliefs, judgments, cultural conditioning, and so forth. The ways we perceive other people are always colored by our perceptions of ourselves, and the ways we interpret situations we find ourselves in are colored by our internal environments. The term "perspective" takes all this into account—it is your particular way of seeing or thinking about something, and the filters that define it.

A perspective is something we develop, usually unconsciously, over the course of a lifetime. But it is also something we can shift and expand through self-awareness and discipline. Becoming a master coach requires embracing a coaching perspective, and this may necessitate that you become aware of, question, challenge, and even reject other perspectives you've habitually adopted. The coaching perspective does not come naturally to most of us. It's a discipline that needs to be intentionally adopted and rigorously practiced. It starts with seeing people as wonderful portraits ready to be transformed into masterpieces. Most of us credit ourselves with an open mind; coaching gives us the opportunity to prove it. Regardless of your personal feelings for the people you coach, adopting this perspective is a choice you will need to make in order to coach effectively.

## THE ART OF SUSPENDING JUDGMENT

In order to adopt the coaching perspective, for a period of time we must suspend our judgments. That doesn't mean we must stop judging people altogether—that would be virtually impossible. Judgment is a natural human behavior; it is how we understand and navigate the chaotic world around us. Our brains are designed to make up stories, giving meaning and coherence to events in our lives. When we meet people, we do the same thing—we make up a story. We instinctively evaluate others to make them comprehensible and fit them into categories that have been created over a lifetime.

Although the concept of judgment has a bad rap in contemporary culture, it is not inherently bad, and not all judgments are wrong. In fact, as psychologist Daniel Kahneman points out,". . . most of our judgments and actions are appropriate most of the time. As we navigate our lives, we normally allow ourselves to be guided by impressions and feelings, and our confidence in our intuitive beliefs and preferences is usually justified. But not always."[7]

Our judgments might be formed on the basis of the other person's actions, or they might have more to do with our own values. They could be based on careful observation, informed insight, or hard-earned experience. But they could also be trig-gered by something as superficial as physical features, something as unreliable as the other person's voice, something as inappro-priate as the color of their skin, or something as unfortunate and unfair as our own mood for the day.

The human brain is hardwired to categorize things, events, and people based largely on surface information. To some extent, this has served an evolutionary function, allowing us to quickly make meaning of a situation and move onto other tasks that require more elaborate cognition. Much of this happens "under the hood" of the conscious mind, as neuroscientist David Eagleman likes to put it. Your conscious mind has only a fraction of the processing capacity that your unconscious mind has, so what arrives in your awareness is a kind of snapshot or summary of the impressions made by your unconscious mind. In simple instances, these summaries can be quite accurate, but when it comes to the complex creatures called other human beings, first impressions can miss the mark quite dramatically.

On the basis of these first impressions, we quickly decide how much we can trust others, how valuable they might be to us, or how much potential they have. Even when we experience peo-ple in just one setting, our minds quickly fill in the blanks. Again, this is part of our mental processing. We need to create a coher-ent picture so we know which box to put people in: threatening or harmless, smart or dull, motivated or lazy, engaged or disen-gaged, interesting or boring, honest or dangerous.

Once we've made up our mind about a person (consciously or not), it's often hard to change our perspective. This is due to what psychologists call "confirmation bias," where we look for information that supports our existing views and selectively ignore anything that contradicts them.

Once again, not all judgments are negative, and not all judg-ments are inaccurate. But we cannot coach effectively through the filter of our judgments. The discipline of coaching demands that, in the moment, we cast aside this compelling instinct to label and measure. In order to do this, we need to consciously recognize our judgments or theories about the other person and consider that we might be completely wrong. What if he is not who we think he is? What if she has an entirely different set of motives, values, and traits?

I know this can be hard. As one of my clients recently exclaimed, "But it isn't just me; the whole department knows this person is that way!" Yes, and the whole department is probably wrong, too. Just as individuals use judgments to understand the world around them, groups also collectively make up stories that help them to make better sense out of the inexplicable entities called people.

The bottom line is that even if your observations are right, it's likely that they are actually inhibiting your ability to help this person move forward. In order to deliberately seek out others' highest potential, the great coach intentionally overlooks their shortcomings and limitations.

This is why I coined the term "Talent" as shorthand for the person being coached. Besides being far more elegant than the awkward alternative, "coachee," it directionally indicates where the coach's focus should be. The essence of the coaching perspective is succinctly captured in that single word, reminding coaches that the person sitting opposite them is not a problem to be solved, but a potential to be unleashed.

Holding the coaching perspective is not easy, but it gets easier with practice. Take a moment to consider the people with whom you work most closely. How do you see them? Be honest—at least with yourself—about your judgments and your labels, your favorites and your write-offs. Then see if you can put them aside, at least for a moment. Try to see your colleagues not as high performers and low performers, sidekicks and thorns in your side, but rather as individuals with wonderfully wide-ranging personalities, talents, and abilities. Can you suspend your internal rating system, if only temporarily, and truly look at these people through softer eyes that see only their possibilities? This does not mean that you need to condone poor performance but rather that you will choose to see it as unused potential. Until you are able to see others through these eyes, you cannot be a truly great coach.

Early in my career, I had the good fortune of working with the organizational development pioneer Dr. Herb Shepard, who taught me to see high performance in people as a direction, not a destination. As a young technologist, I had spent the first few years of my career eagerly measuring the performance of all manner of things—processes, systems, machines, and people—treating them all essentially the same. Through many conversations and much coaching, Herb encouraged me to see human beings in a new light. "Do you really believe that humans were created to be judged on the same scale as machines?" he would ask. One day, in the course of some research I was doing with Herb, I came across the book entitled *Born to Win* by Muriel James and Dorothy Jongeward. The words on the very first page rocked me to the core:

> Each human being is born as something new, something that never existed before. . . . Each person has a unique way of seeing, hearing, touching, tasting, and thinking. Each has his or her own unique potential—capabilities and limitations. Each can be a significant, thinking, aware, and creative being—a productive person, a winner.

Every time I read these words, they resonate on a deep level, affirming human dignity and respecting our individuality. In our hasty judgments of each other, we dehumanize and disrespect our fellow men and women. The master coach brings a profound sense of humanity back into the heart of business by honoring and appreciating every individual for his or her greater—and unique—potential.

What would it take for you to develop that kind of perspective, one that appreciates and recognizes the very best in each person you meet? To set aside your judgments and honor the person for who they *could* be? If you are willing to embrace this one simple yet powerful habit, you will touch people in a profound and meaningful way.

This emphasis on perspective is born out of the understanding that our influence on each other goes much deeper than the words we say. You may speak encouragingly to the Talent, but if you don't believe in them, they will know it and are unlikely to respond with change. As I'll be discussing in more depth in chapter nine, it is extraordinary how self-fulfilling our expectations of others can be. If you don't believe in another person's capacities, talents, and potentials you will never be able to help them flourish. And if you focus only on their shortcomings, their failures, their mistakes, and their weaknesses, chances are you won't make much headway on helping them move beyond them.

There are countless people in today's organizations whose job it is to focus on what is missing from any given situation and to limit losses, fix problems, and fill gaps. But there is a great opportunity for the Leader Coach to stand out as a pioneer for what *is* working and to be a promoter of positive change. The coach's role is not to judge others' performance but rather to be an advocate for their potential.

I always find it fascinating how much time and effort companies invest in judgment-based processes like performance appraisals, and yet how little evidence exists to support their effectiveness. Can you honestly recall a pivotal change in your own performance or career that was the result of a performance appraisal? Did the feedback you received from a supervisor during one of these processes ever inspire you to change the way you function in the organization? Have you ever received a rating that was the motivation to achieve the position you have today? Not likely. I have posed these questions to thousands of leaders and the implication usually stops them cold. They can rarely recall even a single instance when a performance appraisal had a significant influence on their own performance or career, but they continue to blindly inflict these on the members of their organizations. Their response, however, is quite different when I ask them to name individuals who have influenced their careers by believing in them when they did not believe in themselves, or by pointing to potentials they had not yet seen. Most have little difficulty identifying two or three people who in this way have been the stimulus for career-changing and sometimes life-changing decisions.

You can be that person for others—the one who focuses on everything that is right, highlights the positive, sees the unseen possibilities, and turns challenges into opportunities. You can be the one who doesn't try to fix others with negative judgments or limiting conclusions, but instead opens doors for them to develop in unimagined ways. Of course, you cannot make the change for other people. That is in their hands alone. The wise coach recognizes that every individual has the innate capacity to change but will only do so when they, personally, make the decision to do so.

## THE OPTIMISTIC COACH

The optimism of the coaching perspective extends beyond individual potential. I've noticed that great coaches tend to have a positive attitude toward the world and the future—an attitude that is infectious. They are purveyors of hope, an all-too-rare commodity in today's world.

In the midst of the turbulent and fast-changing business environment, and the instability of our globalizing world, it is understandable that many people feel overwhelmed and even despondent. Tossed this way and that by forces larger than themselves, they feel powerless and insignificant. Coaches don't ignore these realities. They understand not just that we are living in times of great change, but that the pace of change is highly likely to keep accelerating in most areas of our lives. But they are not intimidated by this reality. They don't pine for the past. They see the changing world as a wonderful chance to reinvent oneself, contribute at higher levels, and seize opportunities previously unimagined. Even in the face of adversity, they believe that negative circumstances are a temporary and not a permanent condition. In essence, the coaching perspective sees all work, careers, and lives as existing in naturally evolving environments and that people can choose to optimize their experience. Rather than feeling victimized by the shifting world around them, coaches hold the perspective that we always have a choice— perhaps not to control our circumstances, but to control our responses. Helping the Talent learn to make these choices in ways that lead them to ever-greater heights of development is the essence of the coach's work.

Some time ago I was at a consulting skills workshop in San Francisco, and on the first morning of the program we were assigned to trios and instructed to introduce ourselves and ask each other questions in order to get to know each other. After I did my introduction, one in my group, who looked more like a hippie than a consultant, said to me "I would much rather imagine who you could be than to learn about who you are today." I confess that I dismissed him as a weirdo who seemed quite out of place in the workshop. But for some reason his words stayed with me and came alive with new meaning once I began my coaching career. While I greatly enjoy meeting new people and learning about their uniqueness, I now share his point of view, and I see it as central to the coaching perspective. A master coach would always rather imagine who the Talent could be and help them to get there.

William James once wrote that, "Pessimism leads to weakness. Optimism leads to power." Great coaches know this, and derive their power from their positive outlook. Optimism is a

precious combustible substance that provides mental and emotional energy, that converts our hopes and aspirations into kinetic
energy and allows us to glimpse the realization of our ideas in
brilliant Technicolor. Optimism drives us to action. It sets a tone
of hope, vitality, and inspiration for others and for ourselves.

According to Dr. Martin E. Seligman, former president of the
American Psychological Association and Professor of Psychology
at the University of Pennsylvania, optimists have three common
traits. They view adversity in their lives as temporary and specific
(not permeating all other aspects of their life). They view adversity
in their lives as external and not entirely their fault. And they are
not defeated by setbacks. Those who have an optimistic outlook
will roll with the punches, will be more proactive and persistent,
and will not abandon hope. Pessimists, on the other hand, tend
to view adversity as permanent, (unchangeable) and pervasive
(affecting all aspects of their lives). A pessimist views adversity as
more personal (viewing him- or herself as the source of the adversity; that it is all his or her fault). In the face of setbacks or challenges, pessimists are more likely to do worse than predicted and
even give up, while optimists will persevere. Optimism, therefore,
is a crucial component of personal achievement, and is especially
important in times of chaos, change, and turbulence.

There is no doubt that optimism gives one a competitive
advantage. Where others have resigned themselves to the status quo, those with an optimistic outlook seek to take control
of their destiny. They believe that they can have a big influence
on the future—and that belief fuels their optimism, which in turn
fuels their power. Master coaches are motivated by a strong inner
sense of their ability to work with the energy of all situations.
They know that they can deal with whatever hand they are dealt,
when they put in the effort required. This confidence helps them
stay the course, if they deem this beneficial to their desired outcome, and it helps them create an environment in which the Talent also develops resilience and optimism.

So, where does optimism come from? Is it something we are born with or is it learned? For some lucky individuals, being optimistic comes naturally. The good news is that, for those who don't have it naturally, optimism is an attitude that can be learned and practiced. You have a unique power to control your thoughts. This makes you the creator of your inner world. What is your internal dialogue? Are there any patterns that you can detect? Are these patterns increasing your personal power? Do they provide unbounded clarity of mind about your purpose, your desired achievements? Or are they muddying the process by restricting you, by holding you back? If so, what can you do to substitute these internal maps with more viable ones?

One obstacle in the quest for developing an optimistic outlook is the feeling of regret for what has passed. Regret is a mental energy thief and mental energy is essential to optimism and personal power. Dwelling in the regret lane is also immobilizing. Above all, regret clouds our perception of the present and the future. Truly optimistic individuals are able to move on and let go, without losing faith in themselves and in their future. It's as though their vision allows them to see around the corner and what they see there, invisible to others, is better than what is. The coach is driven by the belief that they can make tomorrow better than today—for themselves and for others. And while they expect to receive more, they are not derailed if they receive less. So how do you develop this belief in a better tomorrow and the ability to deal with less than what was desired as situations evolve? The secret to accomplishing this is choosing the somewhat blissful and ennobling state of appreciation, experiencing the power of gratitude, and counting one's blessings.

When coaching clients, I often ask them to list four or five things that they are grateful for, in the moment. I then suggest that they begin their day with this ritual of appreciation. What are your blessings? How many can you list right now? How would your life change if you began your day, every day, from that perspective? Would your outlook become more optimistic?

This may sound like a simple practice, but I assure you it is life-changing. If more people did this one simple thing, I'd be out of business! They wouldn't need coaching because they would be beginning each day with a powerful sense of humility and gratitude. They would arrive at work feeling energized, positive, and ready to have a powerful impact on others.

## A SPIRIT OF CURIOSITY

The best coaches have a strong sense of exploration. Explorers are not only comfortable with the unknown but yearn for it. They are drawn to uncertainty and surprise. In a business culture that likes to reduce everything to measurable, knowable quantities, these qualities provide an important counterpoint. The coaching perspective embraces the unknown as the realm of possibility, the ground from which change can occur.

When coaches look at other people they see them as mysteries to be uncovered rather than problems to be solved. In this sense, curiosity is a fundamental coaching competency. In fact, it is a prerequisite to catalyzing change. It shifts conversations from being routine and superficial to being intense and impassioned, carrying both coach and Talent beyond the familiar with penetrating questions and incisive inquiry. The coach not only believes in the potential of the Talent; he or she is excited to see that potential unfold and fascinated by the question: what more is possible?

Genuine interest in other people—and in what other people can become—cannot be faked. People know when we really want to learn more about them and what is most important in their work and life, and they know when we do not. The good news is that you can develop an explorer's mindset. This is a competency that can be cultivated as you learn to think like a coach. The more you make the effort to suspend your judgments about others and resist labeling people, the more you will awaken a natural appreciation that fosters curiosity. Human beings are fascinating works in progress, and no two are alike. Watching the mystery of human potential unfolding is one of the great pleasures of coaching.

I find it fascinating that adopting the coaching perspective benefits the coach as much as the Talent. When I can truly approach my clients from this perspective, I learn much more from them than they learn from me. I am always inspired by the courage they display as they struggle with their unique challenges. Focusing on the development of another and watching that person reach new heights of performance is a reward like no other. And seeing that person go on to coach and help others develop is the biggest payoff of all.

The great challenge for the coach, however, is to hold the coaching perspective even before the payoff is delivered. This runs counter to the modern mindset, which likes to demand, "Show me! Show me you are trustworthy and I will trust you. Show me that you have potential and I will teach you." It's easy to believe in someone's potential once you've seen it; it's much harder when it has yet to reveal itself. Which brings us back to where we began: *Coaching is an act of faith in people.*

This simple phrase came back to me recently during a conversation with one of my fellow coaches, Jim Boneau. "What's the biggest mistake you've ever made as a coach?" I asked him. Without hesitation, he replied, "losing faith in people too quickly." He paused. "You know, sometimes the coaching conversation just isn't flowing, and the person seems resistant to everything I have to say, and before too long, I've written him off. And then, months later, he shows up again and tells me that the conversation changed his life."

As I reflected on his answer, I thought of times when I too had made that mistake and lost faith in someone's ability to change, only to be surprised when that person came back to me and told me what an impact our conversation had made. The beauty—and the challenge—of the coaching perspective is that you don't often get to see the proof right away. That's why I use the term faith.

Sometimes the shift is instantaneous. You see the Talent transform before your eyes. But many other times you're left unsure if any change will occur, and over what length of time. Ultimately, that is in the hands of the Talent—they have to make the choices and do the hard work of transformation. Your job, as a coach, is to keep the faith.

# 3

# Coaching Is Everyone's Business

*Leadership is everyone's business.*
—JIM KOUZES and BARRY POSNER

**"I** don't need a coach, I'm the CEO!"

Eric Schmidt, Executive Chairman of Google, recalls that this was his initial response to a board member's suggestion that he might benefit from coaching. "Everyone needs a coach," his wise colleague told him. Eric agreed to give it a try, and now he says that was the best piece of advice he ever got.[8]

We tend to think that high-performing leaders don't need coaching, but nothing could be further from the truth. Coaching is not just a remedial approach, reserved for leaders in crisis. In my personal practice, I only coach high-performing senior executives, and every single one of them has proven that they still have a bigger game to play and can make a shift in their performance through coaching.

Great coaches don't see individuals as being at various levels of success. They see everyone as being on a pathway. Even high performers are on a pathway and through coaching, can potentially find a better one, or move forward more quickly. One of the fundamental elements of great coaching is putting aside our judgment of people as "high potentials" or "low performers," because in the moment, none of that really matters. The job of the coach is simply to help the Talent to step up their game, regardless of where they are starting.

So yes, everyone needs a coach. And here's another piece of advice that I think is equally important: *anyone* can coach. Coaching is everyone's business. The beauty of coaching is that it is not a role that is reserved for those with specialist knowledge or in positions of power—anyone, at any level of a business, can act as a coach for those around them.

Coaching is not the exclusive domain of senior leaders and external professional coaches. It does not only flow from the top down; it can occur between peers and even across reporting lines. Although this may seem surprising to those accustomed to a traditional hierarchical model, it's been my experience and observation that often those on the lower rungs of the organizational ladder can very effectively coach people above them. The receptionist can coach the CEO, provided the necessary trust has been established (this will be discussed more in Part II). As powerful as it is, this process is within reach of almost all of us.

Of course, good coaches need training, and to really master the art and science of coaching is a lifelong journey. Untrained coaches who don't understand the role can do more harm than good—stepping over into the role of counselor or teacher and offering too much advice and instruction. Those with strong interpersonal skills are likely to be best prepared for the role, but the most important foundation for an aspiring coach is understanding the nature of the coaching relationship—what it is and what it is not.

Many organizations today are working to equip managers with coaching skills, and that's an important step in the right direction. But there's no reason to stop at the management level. Today's organizations are extremely frenetic and even the most well-meaning and committed managers barely have time to coach their own team members. Extending the coaching role beyond the managerial level can lighten the burden on those who are already overwhelmed and equip others to step up.

Any person in the organization can sit with another person and challenge them to lift their game, encourage them to see new possibilities, confront them with their own potential, affirm their many talents and remind them of how great it feels to do extraordinary work. That's coaching. Coaching is not advising others, providing feedback, teaching skills, and solving problems. These are all important managerial practices but they have a different function. When well-coached, people will solve their own problems, seize their own opportunities, and chart their own futures. This is why a wise leader makes coaching everyone's business.

## FROM THE MOUTHS OF BABES

A friend of mine is a principal at a high school, and some years ago, he invited me to lead a workshop for some of the young people in his graduating class who were taking a business course. I decided to offer our one-day Leader as Coach Workshop, which is an experiential program built around live coaching exercises. To add some depth, I invited some business leaders to join me, all of whom were senior executives from large corporations.

During the workshop, both students and executives took turns coaching and being coached. Who do you think got most out of the program? The students loved it, but the senior executives came away more deeply impacted than any of them had anticipated. The student-coaches sat down to each conversation free of preconceived notions about what questions they should or shouldn't ask. They trusted their intuition and let it guide them in their responses. And they were courageous in sharing their perceptions. One after another, the executives came up to me and reported that being coached by these young people was nothing short of transformative.

This did not entirely surprise me. In fact, I've observed many times how even very young children, in their innocence, can be extraordinarily coach-like, simply by asking questions no one else would think to ask or by offering perspectives that are unencumbered by limiting ideas.

I experienced the power of this kind of coaching directly with a young man in my own company. I was leading a workshop and we had an uneven number of participants, so I stepped in to go through the exercises as a partner for a fairly new recruit—someone who didn't know me or the business very well. At the time, I was struggling with a particular challenge. We wanted to grow our business in a certain sector, and I was stuck with a particular idea about how it should happen. As is often the case in coaching success stories, at some level I knew what I needed to do—I needed to make a real financial commitment to this area of growth. But I was resisting it. As a result of that brief coaching session with my young colleague, I decided to take the leap. I often think back to that day as an example of why everyone needs a coach and anyone can be that coach. That twelve-minute conversation helped to change the course of Bluepoint. Our business today is thriving in no small part because of his courageous coaching.

Do you have the courage to approach a conversation with childlike innocence, bearing the accompanying vulnerability? Can you bring that kind of unguarded directness to your role as coach, ignoring the voices in your head that tell you it must be more complicated? In many situations, the wisdom of experience serves us well, but in coaching it can also obscure the most salient questions.

## CREATING A COACHING CULTURE

As you start to make coaching everyone's business, it will become not just an activity that occurs in scheduled sessions but a culture that pervades your organizational life.

Culture is one of those terms that can be hard to define. I like to think about it as the operating system of an organization—the underlying code that creates its distinctive quality. It's what makes a particular workplace unique. It's the company's essence, its ethos, its character. Much has been written about what creates culture and how to influence it, and much remains mysterious about this intangible but critical dimension of organizational life. Culture is clearly more than the sum of the people who participate in it. There are many tales of companies where the personnel changed dramatically but the culture remained surprisingly consistent. Culture exists both within and between individuals, and has a life of its own that defies attempts to reduce it to individual traits. However, most researchers agree that the beliefs, values, and aspirations that are shared by the most influential people in a company, the senior leaders, play a key role in creating culture.

Culture is something you can observe most readily through its effects—the behaviors and artifacts it gives rise to. But the thing itself is more elusive. You can *feel* it, but its hard to put your finger on exactly what it is and why. My good friend and colleague Bob Johnson, who I've known and worked with for more than thirty years, likes to say culture is "how the people feel about having to go to work every day." He believes he can get a sense of the culture of any organization by just spending fifteen minutes sitting in the reception area.

Although corporate cultures are distinctive and varied—think Goldman Sachs vs. Pixar, or Walmart vs. Whole Foods Market—they quickly become invisible to us when we're embedded in them. If you've been working within a particular culture for years, it can be particularly hard to recognize it—just as you probably don't see the culture within your own family. But think about an instance when you've visited a new family for the first time, such as meeting the parents and siblings of a significant other. Or think about returning to your own family or home country after a long absence. Because you are observing from the outside, so to speak, you are able to see the human dynamics in a way that those who have been part of that culture for a lifetime cannot. You'll find yourself paying close attention to the way people relate to each other, their interactions, their customs, and their cues.

While it can be difficult to pin down exactly what creates an organization's culture, it is relatively easy to see the results. An organization's culture is manifest in its unique norms and practices, the unwritten rules that you may not find in the Employee Handbook, but which anyone who's been there more than a few weeks learns to follow. One of the simplest and best ways of describing culture is one I picked up from a former college professor: "It's the way we do things around here."

A coaching culture is one in which the values, perspectives, and behaviors of the coach have become part of that "way we do things," not just in formal coaching sessions but in informal interactions every day. How do you know when this is happening? Here are some signs you might notice.

## THE 7 CHARACTERISTICS OF A COACHING CULTURE

1. Personal and organizational learning is greatly valued.

2. People are excited about their personal and professional development opportunities.

3. Leaders are seen as trustworthy, selfless, and competent.

4. Promises are readily made and faithfully kept.

5. Difficult conversations are routine.

6. People delight in the success of others.

7. Well-intentioned feedback flows freely throughout the team or organization.

When coaching begins to become widespread in an organization, all these changes and more begin to occur. It might not immediately be apparent where they're coming from, but I can assure you that coaching is playing a significant role. My colleague Joan Peterson recently shared with me a story about a company she worked with where the initial coaching workshops involved only the senior executives and managers. Some weeks later, she rolled out the next level of training for the mid-level teams. Halfway through the session, one man raised his hand and declared, "I knew there was something different about work and about my boss these past few weeks, but I couldn't put my finger on what it was. I just knew that work had become a better place for me." As he went through the training, he realized, "Now, I know what it is! My boss has been doing this with me." Joan and her team continued to hear similar stories as they worked with more and more groups in the business. As coaching becomes part of the culture, it changes the culture.

## THE CHALLENGE OF BEING MANAGER AND COACH

While creating an internal coaching culture has many benefits, I'm not overlooking the challenges involved. To be honest, my job as an external coach is much easier than the job my clients are taking on as Leader Coaches. I'm temporary; I can walk in and ask my clients questions they've never been asked before, challenge people, and raise issues that could never be raised inside the organization. I can invite them to talk about dreams and aspirations never before discussed. The Leader Coach has a much tougher job. He or she has to live with the Talent, day in and day out, and this complicates the coaching relationship.

The Leader Coach has to straddle two roles that have very different requirements. Managers who coach their team members still have to perform all the other supervisory functions, such as providing direction, giving corrective feedback, and monitoring performance. It is indeed a real challenge to have one of your team members openly discuss their shortcomings in a coaching session when they know you'll be judging their performance next week. And it takes a highly trusted and deeply committed leader to be able to, in one moment, give an underperforming staff member direct, well-intentioned feedback about the consequences of their poor performance, and in the next moment, extend the hand of coaching, with no judgment—not as a remedial solution, but simply to help that person learn and function at their very best.

Great leaders rise to this challenge and find ways to be coach-like every day. The test of a true Leader Coach is the ability to shift gracefully between the multiple roles they need to play.

The Coaching Impact Model helps leaders understand how coaching relates to the other activities in which they engage. This simple chart illustrates where coaching sits along a continuum with other very important leadership practices: directing, advising, teaching, and mentoring.

It's important to emphasize that I am not making a value judgment between these activities. They are all critical leadership functions, but they are suited for different circumstances. The determining factor, when it comes to choosing the appropriate form of leadership, is, "Who owns the Agenda?" Think about the "Agenda" as the issue at hand: the decision, the challenge, the opportunity, the Talent's performance or aspirations. If the leaders own it entirely—for example, with non-negotiable agendas like compliance, ethics, and high-level strategies—they will be directing. But as you move along this continuum to the right, the leader has decreasing ownership of the Agenda. When the Talent owns the entire Agenda, a coaching conversation is possible.

While directing, advising, teaching, mentoring, and coaching are all legitimate and important ways of functioning as a leader, the long-term sustainable impact occurs at the coaching end of the continuum. I've asked thousands of participants in our workshops to identify the people who impacted them the most

## The Coaching Impact Model

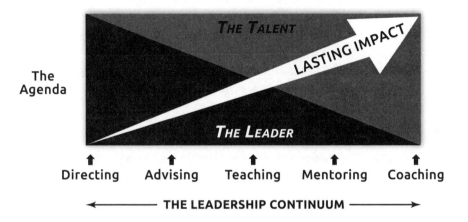

The
Agenda

Directing   Advising   Teaching   Mentoring   Coaching

← —————— THE LEADERSHIP CONTINUUM —————— →

in their career or life. Virtually every one of these people inter-acted with the participant in a coach-like manner; at the far right end of the Leadership Continuum.

Under pressure, leaders tend to drive toward the left side of this spectrum. It takes a lot of courage to give over control of the Agenda to someone else—someone who might make seri-ous mistakes that reflect on you. It also takes more time. Advising and directing can seem so much more efficient in the short term. And the leader's ego is often attached to the role of being teach-er-like and authoritative, dispensing their knowledge and exer-cising their power. Again, it is easier for an external coach like me to give up ownership of the Agenda. I know that I don't have the domain expertise to own it even if I wanted to, and I'm not being held responsible for the performance of those I coach.

Being a Leader Coach is extraordinarily difficult, and I have the utmost respect for those who embrace the challenge. These courageous men and women must move along that continuum all day long, shifting seamlessly from director to advisor to teacher to mentor to coach, and knowing which role is most appropriate in the moment. It's hard to do, but the payoff is significant.

# Making Coaching Everyone's Business: 7 Steps Leaders Can Take

✦✦✦

*The process is surprisingly straightforward but does not come without investment on your part. You need to be personally involved every step of the way. Here are the seven things you need to do:*

1. Strongly encourage everyone in the organization to invite another organization member to coach them. Anyone can coach anyone else. (Yes, I appreciate that some will not get invited and their feelings will be hurt. These people should thank you. Since we need to earn the right to coach others, this is very valuable feedback, even if a bit painful.)

2. Dive into the process yourself. Invite someone in the organization to coach you, and insist that all senior leaders do the same (You will undoubtedly notice that "insist" is a bit stronger than "encourage").

3. Remind your team that anyone can coach anyone. A good coach is a good coach. Don't waste HR's time in the futile pursuit of "good matches" or "chemistry". (And yes, you can coach your boss)

4. Ask people to take on only one coaching assignment at a time. This will ensure that each person will receive the full attention of their coach and will spread the coaching opportunities (and load) throughout the organization. (Please note that this does not absolve leaders from being consistently coach-like with all their team members.)

5. Provide the following loose but important guidelines: Coaching pairs should meet in person or via telephone for 30–60 minutes (this is lots of time for great coaching

to happen) every 2 to 3 weeks (this will keep the momentum going) for 4 to 6 months (this is enough time to develop new performance standards and create new habits.)

6. At the end of every coaching engagement, encourage people to invite a different organization member to coach them. (Yes, there is always another higher level of performance possible and a good coach will not rest until it is found.)

7. Equip everyone in your organization with the skills, perspectives, and approaches necessary to immediately coach at a high level. If you find the right program, this will only take one day, two at the most. Unfortunately, most coach training programs focus an inordinate amount of attention on interpersonal skills such as active listening and providing feedback rather than what it takes to really *be* a coach. It is very important that your people participate in a highly experiential training program that introduces them to the potency of coaching, provides them opportunities to practice real coaching and receive direct feedback on the same. You will also want to make sure that they are fully equipped with the tools necessary to:

   ○ ask questions that pierce through closely held assumptions and mental models,

   ○ constructively confront unhelpful behaviors, practices and attitudes,

   ○ affirm strengths, talents and abilities even if rarely employed, and

   ○ share fresh perspectives no matter how radical.

Stand back and watch. When coaching is seen as everyone's business . . . it can change the entire game!

The magic of a coaching culture is that it is infectious. Any time someone has been well coached, they become more coach-like themselves. Employees at all levels begin to accept ownership and accountability for their work and relationships. They require less daily and direct supervision from managers as they develop their skills and strive to reach their full potential.

# 4

# How People Learn, Grow, and Change

*When you study great teachers . . . you will learn much more from their caring and hard work than from their style.*
—WILLIAM GLASSER, *The Quality School*

Change. It's often described as the only constant in life. Yet for most of us, change can be hard. Many believe that humans are evolutionarily predisposed to resist change because of the risk associated with it. Homeostasis is the evolutionary term sometimes employed to describe the way in which organisms gravitate toward maintaining a level of biological balance. The same can apply psychologically as well. We settle into a way of doing things that feels familiar and that requires limited effort to maintain.

It is common to hear researchers, writers, conference speakers, and the like assert that most people have an ingrained nature that "resists change." Leaders are exhorted to employ all manner of practices and approaches to confront this plague and "drive change" through their organizations. This most often involves creating an exciting picture of a new vision and making sure everyone knows what fabulous rewards await all when the vision becomes a reality. Typically, what follows is lots of talk and lots of meetings and lots of plans and lots of great intentions and then, well, nothing. The notion of driving change through the organization makes leaders feel powerful and in charge, however, the outcomes of most such initiatives are often very disappointing.

The problem with these approaches is the assumption that change is unwelcome, difficult, and instinctively avoided by people. In fact, the ability and willingness to change both ourselves and our environment is one of humankind's most dominant and important traits. Our capacity to create novelty, reinvent ourselves, and strive for new heights is an indelible part of our nature. Think about how we have responded to opportunities and threats throughout the ages. We bob. We weave. We change. We are hardwired to adapt. We'll sharpen a rock when our hands will no longer protect our children. We'll cross treacherous seas when prejudice and corruption stifles our future. We'll elect a president who could have been enslaved at birth if born a few generations earlier. The more neuroscientists learn about the working of the human brain, the more they learn that we yearn for change, for novelty, for anything that will make our lives fresh, better and more exciting. It's time for leaders to embrace the idea that their most important role is not to drive change, but to facilitate the natural desire to change. And one of the most effective ways to do this is through coaching.

## LIFELONG LEARNING

One of the most important outcomes of coaching—perhaps *the* most important outcome—is learning. Here is the key: The master coach is a very effective facilitator of learning without being a teacher.

It used to be commonly believed that most learning and development happened in childhood. One only has to spend a few months with a young child to be awed by the continual change that is occurring in their bodies and minds. But with adults, development is less evident. In fact, until recently, both psychologists and biologists agreed that after the onset of adulthood, very few major changes took place in the human body, psyche, or capacity to learn. Kids went to school; adults got on with the business of living while their bodies and brains remained stable and then began a slow decline. But all that has changed in the past century. Freud's one-time disciples, Erik Erickson and Carl Jung, proposed theories of human development continuing throughout the lifespan, and emphasized the potential for positive change very late in life. Following in their footsteps, a new generation of psychologists began to push the edges of how we understand the adult self and propose that in fact adults continue to develop and have previously unrecognized capacities for learning and change.

Looking back on the past few decades, Harvard psychologist Bob Kegan, who has been one of the more stalwart proponents of this notion of adult development, explains that, "The great glory within my own field . . . has been the recognition that there are these qualitatively more complex psychological, mental, and spiritual landscapes that await us and that we are called to after the first twenty years of life."[9] My work with individuals all over the world fully affirms this basic insight. Adults can, and do, develop in tangible, positive ways and have an innate capacity for change.

In more recent years, it has been heartening to see even the so-called hard sciences come around to this point of view, particularly those studying the enigma of the brain. Biologists had long thought of the adult brain as being pretty much set in its ways, with none of the malleability and flexibility that defined the developing childhood brain.

Now, data has proven this idea to be false. The adult brain is in fact a malleable, always-changing, highly adaptable organism that is responsive to the stimuli we feed it. The scientific term that has been shouted from a hundred magazine cover stories and championed in bestselling books is *neuroplasticity*. And the message of neuroplasticity is an encouraging one—humans can change, we can make new habits, we can develop, we can open up new pathways of action, and forge new connections in the very circuits that make up our brain and mind. In the new light of neuroscience, we are discovering that humans are wired for change.

Despite this wave of newfound appreciation for adult learning and development, the field it is still relatively new. Compared to the study of childhood development and education, there has not been the same degree of research about how adults learn and what environments and teaching styles best support that learning and development. We have much more insight and data when it comes to children. Due to this lack of research, I suspect, there is a tendency to simply default to the type of learning model we are used to—the classic student-teacher model so prevalent in our childhood and adolescent years. But is that really the best model for energizing the adult learner?

There is an emerging body of theory and research that has come to several conclusions about adult learning, which suggest that the answer to that question is a resounding "no." What they reveal is that a model of learning and development that more closely resembles the coaching paradigm would be far better at facilitating the growth of the adult mind.

## HOW DO ADULTS LEARN?

The following five principles represent some of our best current understanding about how adults learn, and are instructive regarding the qualities any coaching context should do its best to include. Drawing on the work of Malcolm Knowles and others, here is my summary of what we know about the Adult Learner.

**1. Optimal adult learning is self-directed.** Adults learn best when they are actively involved in the planning and evaluation of the process. The adult learning environment needs to be more consensual to have maximum effect. Inevitably, this involves a deeper level of communication at all stages of the process. This fits nicely with a coaching context, as the whole emphasis of a coach should be to help the Talent be more powerfully and intentionally self-directed and involved in their own learning and development. True coaching creates greater self-reliance and autonomy. In contrast to models of learning that we associate with childhood and adolescence, a true coach is not creating the path or building a map for the adult learner to adopt. Instead, he or she is focused on empowering, encouraging, and challenging the Talent to discover that path themselves.

**2. Adult life experience is vast.** A good coach always remembers that adult learners bring all their many years of life experience to the table of learning. Often this will include decades of work experience, community building, travel, and family life. The diversity of people's stories may surprise and delight, even shock and confound our expectations. As coaches we want to be aware of and reject the tendency to assume too much about people based on too little. Most people have won victories we might never imagine and made mistakes that are foundational to who they have become. Making space for that vast degree of life experience is a critical component to good coaching. Adult learners will inevitably draw on that life experience in ways that will prove important to their development. As coaches, we can make room for the richness of their journeys and allow them to play a natural role in the unfolding of their learning process.

**3. Adult learning tends to be goal-oriented.** Adult learners are not only more self-directed; they tend to be more serious about acquiring specific skillsets and knowledge. They're thinking, how can this new skill or perspective help me fulfill my role in my work, or perhaps my role as spouse or community leader? For a coach, this focus can be conducive to supporting a healthy learning environment, and it can also detract. Frequently the source of our deepest and most important insights can come from unexpected places. We can't always know ahead of time exactly how and in what specific direction our future development will unfold. A great coach acknowledges the positivity of goals but guards against allowing them to create blinders that prevent the Talent from seeing their situation in novel, out-of-the-box ways.

**4. Adult learning involves practice, experimentation, and engagement.** Too many models of learning, for adults and adolescents, are based on passive listening and simple absorption of information and knowledge. However, research has shown again and again that adults learn much more effectively through practice, experimentation, and engagement than they do through passive listening. That's why I make the distinction that the coaching process is about more than just learning. Teachers are in the learning business. Coaches are in the development business. I like to define development as *applied learning*. The great coach creates a powerful learning environment but does not stop there. The Talent is then challenged to put their learning into action, try it on for size, and then create new habits, practices, and attitudes that will integrate the learning into their ways of being and rewire their brains.

This brings us back to the concept of neuroplasticity. Part of the way we learn new skills and create new habits is by forming new neuronal connections in our brains. Inevitably, this involves a hands-on approach to learning. Over time, as we engage in a new behavior or repeat a new task or make the effort to perform a new skill or even adopt a new perspective, a subtle but powerful new habit is being formed—not just in the psychology of the mind but in the physiology of the brain. As we continue to engage in those new behaviors, those connections become thicker and the habits become stronger. As a coach, understanding the psychological and neurological process of how human beings form new skillsets and mental habits can be helpful. Practice, experimentation, and immediate application of learning help turn what seems like a huge emotional and mental leap into a normal, even routine, part of adult self-development.

As these principles of adult learning reveal, coaching quite naturally lends itself to the optimal process. Indeed, these learning principles are all present in coaching, which is why it is such an effective way to facilitate and accelerate an individual's efforts to learn, grow, and change.

# LEARNING IN COACHING

I often hear people say, "I love to learn," but I believe what they actually mean is that they like to be entertained by novel and exciting ideas. When I speak about learning, it's important to be clear that I don't just mean the acquisition of new information. I'm talking less about "I learned my multiplication tables" or "I learned how to write some new code in HTML" and more about " I learned a new lesson about how to be leader" or "I learned how my behavior impacts my colleagues, and how I can change it." Real learning, deep learning, is hard because it is always highly personal.

In coaching, real learning focuses on two areas: learning about self and learning about self in relation to others. Both of these are difficult because they often require the Talent to not only learn but unlearn! The Talent usually needs to discover that they need to let go of previous conclusions and convictions to make space for new insights.

There is no knowledge like self-knowledge, and authentic growth—the kind that is lasting, meaningful, and impactful—often begins with a deepening knowledge of self. Learning about ourselves means that we discover, maybe for the first time, the values, beliefs, biases, aspirations, and habits that form the core of who we really are. These aspects of self may be familiar in some sense, but many people are unaware of how these aspects of self influence the way they engage the world around them. Learning about self involves bringing those to light and with that light comes a new sense of empowerment and choice. An effective coach understands that self-knowledge and self-empowerment are closely connected.

A related component of learning about self is learning about self in relation to others. How do we perform and engage in the context of a team? What kind of leadership style do we adopt? What type of relationships do we engage in, both at work and outside of it? It is important to understand here that the point is not to judge which aspects of self are good or bad, right or

wrong, positive or negative. Rather the goal is learning, awareness, and perspective, making the connection between what
goes on inside of ourselves and what the results are on the outside. An effective coach can guide the Talent to make these connections in a way that illuminates and inspires them as much as it
confronts them. This will lead to both deeper knowledge of self
and previously unseen avenues for development and change.

The coach's number one job is to facilitate and deepen the
Talent's learning. And the coach is ideally positioned to do this.
While the coach, as I have said before, is not a teacher, he can
facilitate the Talent's learning and join them in the journey of
discovery. *The coach is directing the coaching process, not the
learning process.* This distinction is important. The coach's role is
to challenge the Talent to take full responsibility for creating their
own learning and development, discovering new pathways forward and previously unseen avenues for learning. In order for the
partnership to work, the Talent must be willing to fully engage in
the coaching partnership, but in the end the growth that results
is self-directed.

One of the most important ways great coaches play their
role is in helping the Talent to see and even predict the consequences of their current actions and behaviors, by connecting newly gained knowledge of self with the consequences of
actions in the world. The beautiful thing about this type of direct
knowledge is that it creates a natural motivation to want to learn,
change, and grow that arises from what the Talent is seeing, not
from what the coach is saying.

As I've stated, all adults have had powerful and formative
(and transformative) life experiences that influence how they con-
struct their lives. These experiences are certainly a deep well of
potential insight and wisdom, but the coach also asks the Talent what story they tell themselves about the meaning of those
experiences.. How is that meaning serving their current aspirations for great growth and new learning? An astute coach will

adeptly help the Talent explore and reframe their life experiences for important lessons and insights they can apply to current problems and opportunities.

This aspect of learning, which involves the *unlearning*, or deconstruction, of the Talent's story, is one of the most important aspects of coaching. It is not the job of the coach to create a new story, but to surface contradictions, challenge assumptions, create doubt, offer new perceptions, and make space for the Talent to generate new interpretations and possible alternate realities. This is a major challenge for both the Talent and the coach, as it is a human tendency to eschew uncertainty and drive for "*the* answer." I believe the great coach is able to help the Talent temporarily hold two or more realities alive at the same time so that real, profound learning can occur.

In many ways, the coach's job is to disturb the Talent's sense of equilibrium by keeping their major assumptions, beliefs, and aspirations front and center in the coaching conversations so the Talent can determine what they really want to learn about themselves and about themselves in relation to others.

The master coach creates a conversation environment in which confusion, disorientation, and anxiety are welcomed, nurtured and seen as precursors to learning. This can be difficult for many coaches. We tend to think it is our job to take away the discomfort. Watching the Talent squirm, the critic screaming in my head is often telling me "You must be a lousy coach. Do something. You must be screwing this up. Quickly . . . Say something clever!" The great coach quiets these voices and allows the Talent to sit in their own discomfort and learn from it.

The master coach is also adept at helping the Talent identify the parts of themselves that are holding them back, their self-imposed barriers. When someone is able to take responsibility for obstacles that they may previously have thought to be external, it is an empowering and significant moment when new possibilities suddenly open up.

A critical element of the coach's role is also to help the Talent create strategies to integrate their learning into their day-to-day lives and work. This often means staying at what I call "the ready position," always on the lookout for opportunities to apply newly acquired knowledge. This is where learning becomes development—when we learn something and then *do* something with that learning.

## COMPETING COMMITMENTS

Let's come back to the pervasive myth of people's so-called resistance to change. It certainly appears to be true in many situations, so how can we better understand what's really going on? Some of the most insightful research I've found on this topic comes from the brilliant work of organizational psychologists Robert Kegan and Lisa Lahey. In *Immunity to Change*, they write,

> ". . . the change challenges that today's leaders and their subordinates face are not, for the most part, a problem of will. The problem is the inability to close the gap between what we genuinely, even passionately, *want* and what we are *able* to do. Closing this gap is a central learning problem of the twenty-first century."[10]

Kegan and Lahey's diagnosis of this gap is one I have found to be tremendously useful in my coaching work. They present the theory of "competing commitments" to explain why people engage in behaviors, often unknowingly, that undermine their ability to make changes that they want to make. Rather than concluding that such people are "resistant," they suggest that a more productive way to look at this might be to recognize that most individuals do have a sincere commitment to change, but they are "unwittingly applying productive energy toward a hidden *competing commitment*."

Competing commitments are simply other things we're committed to that come into conflict with the stated intention to change. If we're not aware that we're committed to two different things that are incompatible, we'll find ourselves mysteriously stuck. "No matter how hard and genuinely we may work on behalf of our [first] commitment . . . is it possible we are also working—and with more effective results—in service of a competing commitment?"[11] Living in this state of inner contradiction, they explain, creates a "process of dynamic equilibrium that works with breathtaking power and effectiveness to keep things pretty much as they are."[12]

Our unconscious commitments, they point out, are often forms of self-protection. These are not negative or unreasonable things like "resistance" but their hidden nature makes them tricky. "The problem is not that we are self-protective, but that we are often unaware of being so," they write. "Without accepting responsibility for the forms our self-protection takes, we are inclined to view [the competing commitments] as signs of weakness."[13] And when we see them in others, we can often interpret them as "resistance."

What's powerful about this idea of competing commitments is that acknowledging them shortcuts the blame-and-shame cycle. And most importantly, for coaches, it allows us to work with the Talent to find creative ways to negotiate these seemingly incompatible aspirations. Underlying our unconscious commitments are big assumptions, as Kegan and Lahey point out. Revealing and acknowledging the commitment allows us to question the assumption. Often, those assumptions turn out to be less true than they seem, and we may even discover that when the assumption is removed, our commitments turn out to be more compatible than we thought they were.

While Kegan and Lahey assert that people hold a wide variety of competing commitments, it has been my observation that the range narrows dramatically in the workplace. At work, we are remarkably similar. Most of us share three common, deeply held "competing commitments" and we will only change when we are confident that the new state will satisfy all these commitments. Whether we are the janitor or the CEO, we are profoundly and irreversibly committed to being:

- an important part of the system,
- seen as uniquely competent, and
- free to make our own choices.

Expressed another way, when it comes to our jobs, we don't want to be irrelevant, appear inept, or be significantly constrained by others. This is not deep, complex psychology. While humans are multi-faceted and diverse creatures, we share remarkably similar mental models when approaching our work. In fact, these three commitments are so widely held that coaches can use them as a universal blueprint for very potent conversations.

Here's the good news: People are not naturally resistant to change—quite the opposite. They crave change. They just need help to shed light on their competing commitments, and support to learn and develop in ways that are conducive. This is the coach's job—to see people's potential for change, nurture their desire for it, help them shed light on the obstacles to it, and put it into practice until it becomes habit.

## COACHING, THE BRAIN, AND THE MIND

For many, the brain and the mind are the same thing. It is important for the coach to understand the difference. The brain is an amazing organ. It is by far the most complex organ in the human body and spends every waking and non-waking hour managing the body's central nervous system as well as processing thoughts, memories, ideas, physical movements, and the like. The anatomy of the brain is complex due to its intricate structure of nerve cells and blood vessels. This amazing organ acts as a control center by receiving, interpreting, and directing sensory information throughout the body. It has a physical form that can be studied.

The mind, on the other hand, is amorphous. While it is deeply connected with the brain, it does not exist in physical form. It is, however, the essence of who we are, individually, as humans. The brain is a physical entity; the mind is the place where we experience our sense of self. The brain synchronizes its roughly 100 billion neurons while managing 45 miles of nerves carrying 100,000 messages per second each travelling at 400mph. The mind does none of this, choosing instead to be the vehicle for understanding complexity, creating ideas, feeling guilty, determining meaning, etc. The mind contains everything important to the coach: memory, consciousness, personality, values, aspirations. The coach targets the mind, deepening thinking and feeling.

Neuroscience is the study of the brain and how the nervous system functions. Neuroscientists focus on the brain and its impact on behavior and cognitive functions. It is interesting to note that, in the past couple of decades, through imaging and other research and investigative techniques, we learned an amazing amount about how the brain actually works and how it impacts our cognitive, emotional and behavioral functions. Should this trend continue for the next few decades, and there is no reason to believe otherwise, I suspect that we will discover many more amazing things about the human brain. The same cannot be said of the mind. For the most part, when a neuroscientist makes a discovery about the brain, the research can be generalized across virtually all human brains. This cannot be so with the mind because each of us has a unique one. Like snowflakes, they are similar in beauty but different in composition. Therefore, every coaching conversation is an exploration into the mostly unchartered reaches of the Talent's mind. And what is discovered there is valuable only to them and not transferable to others.

# Top 10 Principles of Learning, Change, and Development

◆◆◆

*Since coaching is fundamentally about facilitating the Talent's learning, change, and development, it is important to understand the principles that underpin these processes.*

1.  We are all stuck, to some degree. Often the things that keep us stuck are habits, attitudes, beliefs and relationships that were once very important to us.

2.  We do not resist change; we resist loss. We are naturally wired to adapt to a changing world.

3.  Our past successes often are impediments to moving forward to a new chapter in our work, career or life.

4.  Everyone has the potential and ability to make choices now that will have a significant, positive impact on their future.

5.  It is the willingness to truly learn that distinguishes a person as having high potential.

6.  Many if not most limitations are self-imposed.

7.  Trying to improve or fix others is a futile effort that usually ends up annoying them and frustrating you.

8.  One sincere expression of encouragement can change a life forever.

9.  The most potent step forward usually involves a very difficult conversation.

10. One never becomes a great leader, doctor, or carpenter. Those we recognize as great in their field are ordinary men and women who wake up every morning and choose the high road toward their aspirations.

# 5

# Ethics and Values in Coaching

*Laws and principles are not for the times when there is no temptation: they are for such moments as this, when body and soul rise in mutiny against their rigour . . . If at my individual convenience I might break them, what would be their worth?*

—CHARLOTTE BRONTË, *Jane Eyre*

Where does the master coach stand on issues of right and wrong? Much of the coaching literature asserts that the coach should steadfastly avoid the role of arbiter of ethics or upholder of a specific set of values. Coaches, we are told, should be neutral. It is not their place to judge the people they are coaching, or impose their own values or beliefs on the process. Particularly when it comes to the field of life coaching, we often hear it said that there is no good and bad ,and that the prime purpose of coaching is to free the person being coached from their self-imposed constraints and inhibitions so they can pursue a better life. The coach, in this scenario, is expected to hold a neutral position and encourage the Talent to make decisions that best serve their interests.

While I agree, as I have argued in this book, that great coaches suspend their judgments that may limit the Talent's view of their potential, I do not support this notion of neutrality. In the first place, it's simply impossible for any human being to be truly neutral. Even if we try to put aside our beliefs and values, they will be felt and communicated at some level. We live and work in communities in which our beliefs, values, and actions significantly impact others, for better or for worse. I believe that part of our responsibility, as members of human society, is to strive to make that impact a positive one. In a coaching relationship, the coach's philosophy of life will inevitably make a deep impression on the Talent. Pretending otherwise doesn't serve anyone. I think that if we take values and ethics out of the picture, we weaken the coaching process, removing much of its inherent power. When we adopt the fashionable notion of unconditional acceptance, we lose the opportunity to be truly catalytic in the life of the Talent.

I am not advocating that the coach impose her personal belief system on anyone. This is one of the greatest sins in coaching. One of the best ways to avoid unconsciously doing this is for the coach to be clear and transparent about the beliefs and values she holds, and, more importantly, as will be discussed in the following chapters, to demonstrate those values in action. And she should recognize that the person sitting across from her has different values, and honor those too.

That being said, while values will vary significantly between communities, companies, families, and individuals, I believe there are a few, high-order values that are universal, part of the way we are wired as humans. The list is pretty much the same in every culture: integrity, compassion, service, equality, and honor. Neither the coach nor the Talent can ignore the fact that adherence to these universal values brings out the best in us as humans.

As coaches, we do the Talent a great disservice when we are not bold in emphasizing the power of these key human values. Granted, we do not live in a black and white world and much coaching is ambiguous and uncertain. We must respect the diversity of people, cultures, and belief systems, and take care not to impose our own beliefs and judgments on others. And yet it is equally important that we do not take this to the extreme of concluding that all values are relative. While it may have begun as a healthy corrective to discrimination and the imposition of one culture's values upon another, this type of moral relativism is problematic.

Relativism asserts there are no absolutes; no universal truths or values but only those that exist in relation to the norms and history of an organization, community, or culture. It's my conviction that there are certain fundamental right-and-wrongs and universal responsibilities to others that apply to all of us, no matter what our race, religion, or belief-system. And these values are not something written in an ancient text or imposed by external moral authorities; they are indelibly etched on the inborn moral compass that exists in every human being. The coach's job is to be true to this compass himself, and to hold the Talent accountable to do the same.

Indeed, the coach's responsibility, in part, is to support the Talent as they work to discover the way in which that inner compass guides the developmental aspirations of their own life and work. The master coach knows that people can only be happy and satisfied if they are living lives that matter. I have occasionally had conversations with clients who share the uncomfortable proposition that their work (and lives) have not have mattered much in the bigger scheme of things. As coaches, we may or may not be able to help people deal with their sense of regret but we certainly can help them fashion work and a life that matters today and in the future.

How one person finds this sense of meaning and purpose won't be the same as the next person. But I suggest that it will have a flavor of those same deeper values that guide human beings at their best.

One of the signs of the presence of this kind of orientation is almost always a greater degree of personal confidence. This is the deep kind of confidence that is not based on ego or bravado, but on a positive conviction of one's own self-worth. That kind of self-confidence is not something we are born with; rather I have come to believe that it is our adherence to certain ethics, principles, and standards of behavior as well as our aspiration to embody these deeper universal values, explicitly or implicitly, that creates a true foundation of self-worth. In the end, that is a prerequisite for all coaching.

## THE COACH'S PHILOSOPHY OF LIFE

I'm not a philosopher but I've spent much time reflecting on questions of morality, ethics, and values. Through this reflection, I've come to learn that there are three critical principles that are universal and should be touchstones for our work as coaches.

1. Life is a gift and comes with the inescapable responsibility to live it well, regardless of your particular perspective or belief system. The pursuit of happiness, adventure, learning, love, worship, contribution, and so on is not optional—it is the essential purpose of our existence. Throughout the coaching process the commitment to living life well needs to be omnipresent.

2. The pursuit of happiness described in the first principle cannot come at the expense of others. We need to pursue our own best lives while not depriving others of the opportunity to do the same. The often conflicting demands of #1 and #2 are the source of many of the dilemmas in coaching conversations.

3. Life only has meaning when it is used to help others achieve #1. Each of us has an unwritten social contract with others to not only do no harm but to help them accelerate their own pursuits. We, as humans, only exist in relationship to others. Our existence is interdependent and interconnected. In every major spiritual and religious tradition—from Christianity to Buddhism to Sikhism to Islam to Hinduism—we find variations on the theme "Life only has real meaning when spent in service of others." This truth has been enshrined in human art, religion, and philosophies throughout history.

If the Talent is a relatively stable, mature human being, and not a sociopath, these foundational values are well within their reach and the master coach should not hesitate to uphold them as a requisite framework for the coaching engagement. Coaching can only have a sustained, positive outcome when both the coach and the Talent embrace such a framework. Of course, the coach cannot force these values upon the Talent. But he can share them clearly and persuasively, and demonstrate his own commitment to them in all conversations. Remember, the Talent is always judging the coach and may be significantly influenced by his behavior. He can also help the Talent to identify their most important values and encourage them to explore how they can enhance their work, career and life, and sense of self-worth by pursuing the most noble of these. The coach brings an optimistic bias into the conversation about the benefits of having an agenda of doing good in the world.

Coaching is not values-neutral. And one of the strong biases of the coach is the belief that humans do better in life not just when they win but when they do good. So, for example, if I am coaching someone who desperately wants a promotion, I'm happy to work with him on that, but I'll also encourage him to think about how he can contribute and help others in the process of getting there.

If the Talent is not striving to live these noble values, the coach's first step is to help the Talent predict the consequences of their choices on themselves and others and confront them with this. Should they choose to take a "low road," they should do so knowing that they are likely choosing pain and misery for themselves and others and when they choose a high road they are choosing strength and satisfaction. If the Talent refuses to embrace these essential philosophies of life, ultimately the courageous, principled coach will withdraw from the relationship.

I believe that the three principles set out previously in the Coach's Philosophy of Life offer a robust and broad framework for engaging in all kinds of everyday dilemmas. When they have been agreed upon by coach and Talent, the coach has permission to use this framework as a reference point as he helps the Talent navigate choices. "Is this good for you? Will it do no harm to others?"

# PART II

# The Master Coach Model

**CHARACTER:**
*Earning the Right to Coach*

**CONNECTION:**
*Creating Partnerships for Inquiry, Learning,
and Change*

**CONVERSATION:**
*Engaging in Dialogue that
Generates Possibilities and Pathways*

# CHARACTER:
# Earning the Right to Coach

*From the Son of Heaven down to the mass of the people,
all must consider the cultivation of the person the root
of everything besides. It cannot be,
when the root is neglected, that what should
spring from it will be well ordered.*

—CONFUCIUS, *The Great Learning*

You may have a desire to coach, but the decision to coach is not yours alone. Becoming a Leader Coach requires that two choices be made. First, one must choose to invest time and energy to help another person create significant change. Second, the Talent must choose to include the coach in their efforts to change. Coaching cannot happen unless another person allows you to do so. You must earn the right to coach, and you can only do so through the quality of your character.

The minimum requirement is that the Talent accepts you as a coach. However, your coaching will be more effective if you are welcomed into the relationship. And the most powerful coaching happens when the coach is not merely accepted, or even welcomed, but *invited* by the Talent to be a partner in their developmental journey. While you may start your coaching career by promoting your services as a coach, you will know when you have become a master coach when people are lining up to have conversations with you.

What inspires another person to invite you to engage with them in the challenge of personal change? What promotes the necessary trust to bind the coaching relationship? It's not just your credentials, your track record, or your position. It's something that is at once more intangible and yet at the same time quickly apparent to most people. To put it in simple terms, it's *who you really are.*

As a Leader Coach, you are the instrument of change. As discussed in chapter one, you are the ultimate instrument of coaching and no book or manual can take precedence over your own personal presence. Many of our life-changing moments occur when someone we trust has a conversation with us about something that is deeply personal. In this sense, all coaching is personal, and who you are will have more of an effect on your ability to facilitate exceptional performance in others than any theory or technique. It will be through your own actions and attitudes that others will identify you as someone they want to be coached by. I use the term "character" as shorthand for this complex of personal values, traits, motives, and habits that make up *you.* Earning the right to coach is a matter of character.

Like it or not, our character is always on display. Human beings are deeply attuned to each other, and no matter what someone says, we are also paying attention to who they are and how they are. Without realizing it, we move through our daily lives assessing everyone around us, attempting to detect sincerity and insincerity, and adjusting our behavior accordingly. We all have the instinctive ability to sense another person's motives, to evaluate their integrity, and to weigh up their trustworthiness. How do you measure up?

Executive coach Charles Feltman defines trust as "choosing to risk making something you value vulnerable to another person's actions,"[14] while distrust is the perception that "what is important to me is not safe with this person in this situation."[15] These definitions are particularly salient when it comes to understanding the dynamics of trust in the coaching relationship. In this case, the "something of value" is nothing less than the Talent's dreams, hopes, fears, anxieties, and sense of direction, in work and in life. So feeling safe takes on a heightened importance when we consider whether or not we want another person poking around in some of the most sensitive and important areas of our performance and career. "Does he respect me?" "Is she someone I can rely on?" "Will he have my best interests at heart?" These are the questions the Talent is asking that determine whether or not you earn the right to coach.

We all have trust issues, and there is nothing wrong with that. It is the way we are wired so we can protect those things that are most precious and most fragile; our fears, our needs, our self-image, our fantasies, our passions, and so on. We are hard-wired to be self-defensive. And since coaching is always personal to some degree, we instinctively avoid coaches with whom we do not feel safe. This is true even at the most senior level of organizations. Remember: the fact that someone is guarded is not a sign of weakness; it is an inevitable part of the human condition. In the coaching relationship, the burden of trust rests not with the talent but with the coach. Coaches need to feel it is their job to actively earn the right to engage in the coaching relationship and conversation.

The master coach looks in the mirror and courageously subjects him or herself to a character assessment. "Would I feel confident engaging in a wide-ranging, truthful conversation about my own development with that person?" "Do I inspire the trust necessary for others to want to share their most daunting problems and ardent dreams?" "What are the qualities that would earn me the right to coach others?"

Leaders, in particular, when they decide to become coaches, often assume that the role can just become part of their job description, along with hiring, firing, performance review, and so on. But coaching doesn't work like that. It's not something we can claim the authority to do *to* another person. It is a peer-to-peer relationship into which the coach must be accepted, welcomed, or better yet, invited. Great coaching often involves exposing treasured aspirations, exploring the scary territory of unfulfilled expectations, claiming talents that have been kept hidden, owning up to the ways one is selling oneself short, making bold new promises, charting risky new courses of action. These are not things we will do with just anyone. These are things we will only do with someone who we believe truly cares about us, is trustworthy, and has something important to offer.

Sadly, when I speak on the topic of coaching, the first question I often hear is not, "What's the most potent thing I can do to improve my effectiveness as a coach?" but rather, "What can I do with all the people on my team who are uncoachable?" The honest answer is one that most leaders don't want to hear: "In all likelihood, it's not that they don't want coaching; they just don't want coaching from you!"

Coaching requires a special relationship and an extraordinary conversation in which people explore ways they can create significant change in their work, careers, or lives. At its best, it can only be described as intimate. The idea that some people are uncoachable emanates from the myth that coaching is something we do *to* others. It's not. It's a powerful, performance and career changing process that we do *with* others. We may call ourselves coaches. We may offer ourselves as coaches. We may encourage others to avail themselves of our coaching. But we can't unilaterally impose ourselves on others as coaches. No matter how senior we are, no matter how interpersonally skilled we are, no matter how experienced we are, we still have to earn the right to coach.

Unfortunately, the notion that coaching is something we do to others is propagated by a plethora of coaching books and training programs that naively assert that leaders simply need to engage in what amounts to a series of interpersonal steps designed to entice others into coaching conversations. "State your intentions, express confidence in the person, listen actively, provide balanced feedback, co-create an action plan." The list goes on. These are good leadership practices, but they will not get you invited into a real coaching relationship.

Think about a person who has been particularly coach-like in your life. Now, consider the following questions: How did this person become important to you and earn the right to be your coach? Why did you welcome this person into your life, allow him or her to talk about the things that were most important to you at the time? Why did you hear this person above all others in your world? When I reflect on these questions myself, I realize that the people from whom I have sought and continue to seek coaching have a strong values-orientation. They are clear about their personal values and live them consistently. First and foremost, they are authentic. They exude a strong sense of meaning and purpose.

My own great coaches also have a wonderful blend of humility and self-confidence. They have a healthy level of self-esteem— one of the reasons they are able to engage with me authentically is that they do not need to work on their own ego issues at my expense. Finally, my best coaches enter into our relationship with noble intention; they genuinely care about me and my success and will sacrifice some of their own needs so as to attend to mine. In the chapters that follow, we will explore these various character attributes of the master coach.

The Greek philosopher Heraclites is said to have written that "character is destiny," but happily, character is not fixed, and therefore, neither is your destiny. Rather, character can be understood as a deeply imprinted set of habits that have become set in their course through a lifetime of repetition. Such habits are not easy to change, but new ones can be formed through dedication and hard work. "Character is a set of dispositions, desires, and habits that are slowly engraved during the struggle against your own weakness," writes David Brooks in *The Road to Character*.[16] The master coach masters him or herself to become worthy of serving others.

# THE ECONOMICS OF CHARACTER

✦✦✦

Interestingly, strength of character in business leaders is not only correlated with better relationships and nicer corporate cultures. It also shows up in the bottom line, according to a study by KRW International, a Minneapolis-based leadership consultancy. The researchers defined character through four moral principles—integrity, responsibility, forgiveness, and compassion—which they considered to be universal. In anonymous surveys, they asked employees at eighty-four US companies and non-profits to rate how consistently their CEOs and management teams embodied these four principles. When they looked at the CEOs who were rated most highly on these character traits, they found that over a two-year period, their average return on assets was 9.35 percent—compared with an average of only 1.93 percent from those who got low character ratings. So remember, character counts—and perhaps more than you might think. As KRW cofounder Fred Kiel commented in *Harvard Business Review*, "I was unprepared to discover how robust the connection really is."[4]

# Top 10 Qualities of Great Coaches

**+++**

*Does this list describe you? Great coaches:*

1. **HAVE A SPIRIT OF GENEROSITY.**
   They liberally share their time, attention, and energy with others.

2. **SEE THE BEST IN OTHERS.**
   They choose to look past the shortcomings of others to focus on their positive qualities, even if deeply hidden.

3. **HAVE HIGH SELF-ESTEEM.**
   They feel good enough about themselves that they do not use the coaching relationship to feed their egos.

4. **ARE EMOTIONALLY MATURE.**
   They are keenly self-aware, understand how to manage their emotions and are able to create substantial relationships with others.

5. **ARE INTERPERSONALLY COURAGEOUS.**
   They boldly confront those they coach and seek the path to truth in all conversations.

6. **HAVE UNCOMMON COMPASSION.**
   They understand the struggle and pain that often accompanies personal learning and change.

7. **ARE LIFE-LONG LEARNERS.**
   They have voracious appetites for new knowledge and self-development.

8. **ARE STRONG ENOUGH TO BEND.**
   They have a unique blend of flexibility and resilience that allows them to weather the disappointments, setbacks and conflicts inherent in the coaching process.

9. **HAVE AN ACCEPTING NATURE.**
   They recognize and silence their judgmental voices that are a natural part of the human condition.

10. **HAVE A PERPETUAL OPTIMISTIC BIAS.**
    They help the person being coached see that they have the power to create a tomorrow that is better than today.

# 6

# Authenticity

*To be nobody but myself—in a world which is doing its best, night and day, to make me somebody else—means to fight the hardest battle any human can fight, and never stop fighting.*

—e.e. cummings, *"A Poet's Advice to Students"*

To be nobody but myself—in a world which is doing its best, What values do you look for in a coach? I recently surveyed businesspeople about this question, and their number one response was definitive: more than 80 percent chose "honesty and integrity" above all other listed values. Another way I often hear this expressed is "authenticity." These three terms comprise the foundation of human character and they are critical for a coach who seeks to inspire trust in others.

While used frequently, none of these terms are necessarily easy to define. They are human qualities that fall into the "I'll know it when I see it" category. We instinctively recognize them in others, even if we can't say precisely why or how. And we place our trust in others—or not—based largely on this perception.

If you are a leader, I am sure you're already aware of the indispensability and the fragility of trust. If people do not trust you, everything else you do becomes inconsequential. Forget trying to be inspirational, coach-like, innovative, supportive, a team player, or a visionary. If you don't have people's trust, they may do what you tell them because you have positional authority, but they will never give you their best work. And you will definitely not be welcomed into the trust-based relationship between coach and Talent.

In our troubled times, organizations and their leaders are facing a crisis of trust. Most leaders will readily agree that earning and keeping the trust of others is critical to their effectiveness. It is quite possibly the single most important prerequisite for leaders at all organization levels. Unfortunately, it can also be the most fragile. As Warren Buffett famously said, "It takes twenty years to build a reputation and five minutes to ruin it." In the current economic climate, with trust in institutions at an all-time low, confidence in organizational leadership has also been shaken to the core.

Against this backdrop of suspicion, leaders must strive even harder to be trustworthy. And they face a difficult predicament: the more senior you are in your organization, the more difficult it is to be seen as authentic. The more you rise up the corporate ladder, the more you will be in the spotlight and the more visible your actions. And just when you need it the most, the helpful feedback and coaching that you probably received earlier in your career will become increasingly rare. Being authentic, as a manager or leader, takes unusual courage and commitment. Yet it is essential.

Authenticity is a vastly overused term in today's organizations, and may have lost its edge as a result. But it stands for something powerful and rare. If you think you've achieved it, you're probably underestimating its meaning. For all but the rarest of great leaders, authenticity is an aspirational value.

Authenticity is the currency of trust. We instinctively trust people who we deem to be real, genuine, and sincere. Those who are transparent with their weaknesses, who have the courage to be vulnerable, and who admit their mistakes honestly are far more likely to gain our trust than those who try to project an image of perfection. And yet authenticity is a challenge, for all of us.

Authenticity is not something we ever fully achieve. It is a life-long battle—a war fought both inside and outside ourselves. Why is this so hard? In part, it is because from a very young age, our culture actually encourages us to be somewhat inauthentic. We're socialized to suppress our emotions, to project the images we think others want to see, and to fit in rather than stand out. We live in a world that tries to seduce us into forsaking who we really are for someone who others tell us we should be. Be sexy. Be nice. Be tough. Be a winner.

Vulnerability can be uncomfortable and dangerous—intensely so—and we instinctually avoid it. Sometimes the desire to appear smart or competent can override an honest admission that we don't know how to do something, or we don't have the necessary skills. Being ourselves might seem like the most natural thing in the world, but for many of us, it takes great courage and conviction, particularly when we are surrounded by the clamor of others' opinions and demands. The great American thinker Ralph Waldo Emerson speaks beautifully to this challenge in his classic essay *Self Reliance*, where he writes, "It is easy in the world to live after the world's opinion; it is easy in solitude to live after our own; but the great man is he who in the midst of the crowd keeps with perfect sweetness the independence of solitude."[18]

## MARKERS OF INTEGRITY

So what are these elusive but essential attributes we call integrity, honesty, or authenticity? However we define these lofty moral terms, one thing is clear. As leaders, we are under constant scrutiny, continuously scanned for the qualities these terms point to and judged as trustworthy or not on their basis. I have had the great honor of working with a handful of leaders who have distinguished themselves in this dimension. While these leaders differ significantly in things such as personality, ambitions, and beliefs, they do share four apparently sacrosanct qualities. These exceptional people:

- are very clear on their values and these are evident in everything they do.
- are guided by a strong internal ethical perspective.
- take full responsibility for the consequences of their decisions and actions.
- truly value others.

The above is an impressive list, one that can be very challenging. However, the good news for those who seek to become master coaches is this: these qualities are within the reach of all of us!

## INTEGRITY: VALUES IN ACTION

One of the critical components of integrity is that people have a clear set of values and are firmly committed to living those values in all aspects of their lives. Their actions match their words, and their words and actions are congruent regardless of the circumstances. Whether we meet them at the grocery store, at the office, or at a party, they are essentially the same person. When someone is consistent with themselves in this way, we are much more likely to trust them. As Shakespeare's Hamlet said, "To thine own self be true, and it must follow, as the night the day, thou canst not then be false to any man."

Most of us, if asked, could probably state our values. It is much easier to talk about values than to actually do something about them. The challenge becomes apparent when we take an honest look at whether our lives reflect those values, in terms of how we allocate the precious resources of time, money, energy, and attention. Gloria Steinem is said to have remarked, "We can tell our values by looking at our checkbook stubs." Very true, although these days it would be our credit card statements. We can also tell our values by looking at our calendars. For example, I might declare that my commitment to family is my highest value, but if I look at how I am choosing to spend my time, I would have to admit that it doesn't add up. Sometimes a better question to ask is, based upon my actual behavior and choices, what would others say I value? Then I can ask myself, are those the values I want to be known for?

Integrity begins when we start accepting who we really are. Coming to accept yourself and be honest about your actual values releases significant personal power. Upholding untruths and false appearances to ourselves and to others takes a great deal of energy. When you become more integrated, you stop wasting energy and you will be surprised at how strengthened you feel. As the great physicist Richard Feynman once said, "The first principle is that you must not fool yourself and you are the easiest person to fool."[19]

Of course, some values are not easy to accept, and you may not like the person you are. In this situation, to have integrity means to sincerely strive to change rather than going back to pretending. If the values you see reflected in your choices and actions do not sit comfortably with you, there may be some hard work ahead of you. Identifying those values you hold most dear, and aligning your life with those values is an essential human challenge that great coaches grapple with. For most, this is a lifelong journey.

In the coaching relationship, the Talent should never have to guess what's important to the coach or what his words really mean. A great coach's values are clear, and they influence everything that occurs in the coaching conversation. This does not mean that the coach requires the Talent to adopt his values. It does, however, mean that the Talent knows what is important to the coach, and can trust him to be honest and consistent. The Talent does not even need to agree with the values of the coach; if the coach lives out his values, he will engender the respect necessary to earn the right to coach another.

The master coach desires to be genuine in all she does. She sets her course and holds it, no matter how the winds of the day blow against her. She bears the marks of authenticity earned over time as she steers faithfully according to those inner values that she knows are right and true for her. Those marks are evident to all around her.

The master coach stands out as one who is so committed to his values that he is prepared to pay the price for authenticity. That price might be financial, it might be social, or it might be emotional. Perhaps you're offered a lucrative business opportunity, but it requires that you compromise on something you value deeply. Can you walk away with your head held high? Or let's say you gave your word and it becomes costly to keep it. Can you be true to your word, even if it hurts? If you promised to attend an engagement, and a better, more interesting invitation comes your way, are you prepared to honor your acceptance of the first event? Keeping your word sounds good, but oftentimes it's not easy.

This is not to say there won't be situations in which you change your mind about what's important. If you do, maintaining your own integrity and the trust of others requires that you communicate early and clearly that you have shifted perspective and let people know that you are now committed to something different. Being honest about changes in yourself builds your authenticity with others. The question oft asked of the Talent needs first to be answered by the coach: "What have you said 'yes' to in the past that you no longer mean"?

Integrity is not self-righteousness. It's not something for which we seek applause or expect popularity. It is not about comparing ourselves with others, nor is it about what others think of us. What really matters is what we think of the person we see in the mirror. That's why it's often said that the true test of integrity is who are you when no one is watching. It's all very well to live up to your values when you're being watched, but what do you do when you're alone? Those are the moments when you choose to either be true or to betray yourself, in big or small ways. Sometimes, you will be the only one who knows when you have sold out your core values or failed to live up to your own standards. Authenticity starts and ends with not letting yourself down.

Every time we fail to live by our own values and highest standards, we chip away at our self-respect. And yet, no matter how often we betray our core values, we can never escape the person in the mirror (though we may give it our best shot!). Like it or not, coaching others to their best performance requires us to expect the best of ourselves as well.

The paradox of the quest for authenticity and integrity is that although at the deepest level it is between you and yourself, ultimately these are not traits we can claim for ourselves. It is others who determine if we are authentic, if we have integrity, if we are deserving of trust. We can only do our best to be worthy of those accolades.

## JUST HOW HONEST?

Honesty is closely related to integrity; it is an essential prerequisite to an effective coaching relationship. But it's a rare commodity, particularly in the business world. Think about it—how often in organizations do we tell only part of the truth (that part of the story that enables us to avoid offending someone or that allows us to skirt the embarrassing issues at hand)? How often do we tell people what we are really thinking, feeling, wanting? Are we tempted to avoid any truth that makes us uncomfortable?

Is truth an absolute? That is a philosophical point that needs a far more academic forum than this to be properly debated. What I do know is that our ability as human beings to recognize truth and articulate it is neither consistent nor absolute. We can only view the world from our own unique perspective, and when we speak, we do so from that worldview. One way to look at it is that we function within a self-determined range of honesty. Our conscience takes the liberty of telling us when we have held something back that should have been spoken or when we have lied outright. Of course, honesty is not about saying everything that we think, but it is about being true to who we are and sharing what we truly believe. This is much more difficult than it would seem. Honesty begins with us, which begs the questions: How much do I know about myself? How self-aware am I? Am I being honest with myself right now?

Have you ever noticed how some people are so comfortable in their own skin that they can talk about their mistakes quite openly and freely? They embrace their checkered past and view it as a part of the wonderful tapestry of life. As coaches, they bring this courageous transparency to every session and readily earn the Talent's trust because they are honest about who they are. They recognize that it was usually their failures, rather than their successes, that spurred their greatest growth. The road may have been bumpy and meandering for them, but they now have a wealth of wisdom to offer and are not constrained by continually holding up an image of their life that is false. They are free to be themselves and put their whole self at the disposal of the Talent.

This kind of transparency is a learned habit but imperative for the coach. Over time, you will become comfortable with simply being your authentic self in the conversation and will find people drawn to you as a coach. You will shift from feeling somewhat awkward or embarrassed to feeling at peace with yourself and your role in the relationship. And you'll discover that your transparency invites the same in the Talent. It's infectious. When you open up and are vulnerable first, you make others feel safe to take the risk of opening up to you. As Scottish theologian Joseph Barber Lightfoot wrote, "There is no persuasiveness more effectual than the transparency of a single heart, of a sincere life."

## ACCOUNTABILITY: A DOUBLE-EDGED SWORD

As a coach, you are continuously on display, and those you coach will know whether or not you take full responsibility for your own actions and the consequences of those actions. One of the critical roles of the coach is to hold the Talent accountable, but to do so, coaches have an obligation to demonstrate a high level of personal accountability in their own lives. Great coaches exude a unique sense of personal responsibility. When something goes wrong, they don't blame others; rather, they examine their own choices and accept responsibility for their part in the results. That doesn't mean that they think that everything comes down to them. They accept that many aspects of the environment and other people are beyond their control. They simply are very clear on their boundaries. They are at the same time fully and actively responsible for their own part in the outcome of any situation. And most importantly, this is where they focus their time and energy: on their part in the relationship or the piece that they control. The great coach does not waste energy complaining or blaming but instead seeks to constructively find their own best possible response to any situation—something that is always entirely within their purview.

## SELF-MASTERY AND THE GIFT OF CHOICE

"Not being able to govern events, I govern myself," wrote Michel de Montaigne. The essence of character-building, as I understand it, rests on this simple yet profound insight, which has been echoed by many of history's great minds. Self-mastery has always been a core precept of the men and women who stand out in all fields of human endeavor. They have recognized that while we cannot control what happens to us, we can control our own *responses* to what happens to us. Even in the most dehumanizing circumstance imaginable, the Nazi concentration camps, the great thinker Victor Frankl affirmed this core principle: "The experiences of camp life show that man does have a choice of action. . . . Man *can* preserve a vestige of spiritual freedom, of independence of mind, even in such terrible conditions of psychic and physical stress. . . . Everything can be taken from a man but one thing: the last of the human freedoms—to choose one's attitude in any given set of circumstances, to choose one's own way."[20]

Neuroscientists call this "response flexibility." As neurobiologist Daniel J. Siegel writes, this important prefrontal function "enables us to pause before responding as we put a temporal and mental space between stimulus and response and between impulse and action." That space is critical. In that space we can engage the power of choice and become masters of ourselves. "From a neurobiological perspective," Siegel explains, "this space of the mind enables the range of possibilities to be considered, to just 'be' with an experience, to be reflected upon, before engaging the 'do' circuitry of action. Response flexibility offers the individual a way of choosing to be the 'wisest self' possible in that moment."[21]

I was reminded afresh of the power of this idea about a year ago, when I was leading an Advanced Coaching Skills Workshop for the biopharmaceutical company Celgene in New Jersey. Towards the end of the workshop, one of the exercises required the participants to reflect on the most important tenets underlying their approach to coaching and write a brief Personal Coaching Credo that captured this sentiment.

As each participant read their credo aloud, I was impressed by the clarity of thought and the depth of commitment. But one in particular stood out. It came from Patricia Wetzel (known as Trish), an executive with Celgene who not only has amazing leadership skills but also a genuine passion for coaching. Her credo was only five words long: "There is always a choice!" After she read these words, a thoughtful, reflective silence fell over the room that I believe was the most important learning moment of the day. Although the words were ones we had all heard many times, in the context of the workshop, they struck us as being remarkably profound.

This idea, this Credo, is a treatise on the wonder of life itself. It not only guides but also fuels the entire coaching process. Every moment presents a new choice. The present is always fresh. Choice is a powerful thread that runs through every conversation and the great coach always keeps it in front of the Talent. There are many circumstances that the Talent cannot control (being born into a poor family, the market tanks, the company transfers you, you lose someone close to you); but the Talent can always choose their reaction to these circumstances, their attitude, their next steps.

The master coach is master, first and foremost, of himself. He is choosing, in every moment, to act according to his highest values and most noble intentions. He is also curtailing his tendencies to behave in ways that are inconsistent with his values and beliefs and restraining himself from letting his own needs get in the way of satisfying the Talent's needs. He may choose to overcome his need to be liked in order to ask a difficult question or confront the Talent. Coaching is all about choice. The coach is engaging his own power of choice, and in so doing, becomes available to help the Talent make the best choices possible.

The ability to choose is an extraordinary source of power that often remains untapped. Many of us live semiconsciously, bouncing from stimulus to response without pausing for breath. For the master coach, creating that space for choice and using it wisely is a daily practice. It accompanies every breath they take. In every encounter or event, you can decide, as the great conductor Benjamin Zander puts it, to "turn your attention away from the onslaught of circumstances and listen for the music of your being."[22] What music do you choose to play? Where are your choices leading you? Is it where you want to go? And who are they allowing you to be?

The power of choice does not only apply to action; it also applies to attention. Just as your decisions about what to *do* are important, so too are your decisions about where to put your valuable attention. You have tremendous power when you consciously decide what you will give attention to, and what you will no longer give attention to. Where is your internal focus? What occupies the biggest real estate in your mental space? Does it serve you well?

Through the power of choice and self-awareness, you can not only begin to think and act more deliberately and wisely but become a different person than you are accustomed to being. We all carry within us a mental model of who we are. But all models are a simplification of reality, and are needed to turn the complex into the simple. We are infinitely more complex and vast, more filled with a possibility of being than our mental models can possibly ever represent. The model of ourselves that we carry in our minds is in fact a straight-jacket, one that shapes our perceptions of ourselves and limits us; it places invisible, yet impenetrable, boundaries on what we think we can do, on what talents we use, on what powers we have. As you widen the space between stimulus and response, we have the opportunity to challenge the thinking patterns and behavioral patterns that restrict us, and to become more than we could have imagined.

# 7

# Self-Esteem

*I hold a beast, an angel, and a madman in me and my enquiry is as to their working, and my problem is their subjugation and victory, downthrow and upheaval, and my effort is their self-expression.*

—DYLAN THOMAS, Letter to Henry Treece

It can be more than a little frustrating to the aspiring coach that the journey to excellence starts within. It starts with the very personal struggle against that critical voice that we all have—that voice that tells us that despite any accomplishments we have had, we just got lucky. We are not very talented or special in any way. And the worst part is, someday everyone we know will discover this. We will be found out, and the jig will be up.

Confusion, disorientation, and anxiety are near constant companions in the coaching process. Our natural inclination is to want to make these go away. I am no different. My inner voice (called the "Critic" or "Gremlin" in other literature) is screaming at me "You must be a lousy coach. Look at what's happening! You are really screwing up. Save him. Quickly, think of something to do." The great coach quiets this soul-crushing voice and sits reflectively, allowing the Talent to work through their demons and toughest issues, never taking ownership of them nor seeking to avoid or ignore them.

The great coach holds a singular deep conviction: *I am okay.* This does not mean the coach is arrogant, narcissistic, or has no more learning or growth to do, but that he or she has established a healthy self-esteem and is not unduly troubled by self-doubt and insecurity.

This self-esteem is absolutely necessary, because only a coach who is not worried about herself can be fully dedicated to helping the Talent. Only a coach with nothing to prove can authentically put aside his agenda and focus on what is best for someone else. Only a coach who has let go of the need to be liked or admired can take the risk to confront another in the ways that create breakthroughs.

Without healthy self-esteem, the coach will not be able to model the kinds of learning, confidence, and personal development that are essential in coaching. He will likely avoid the scarier kinds of dialogue because of a lack of inner confidence. He will not have the courage and energy to participate in intense conversations because He will be caught up in concerns about himself. He will use the coaching process to satisfy her own ego, even in very subtle ways, at the expense of the Talent.

People with healthy high self-esteem are easy to be around. They don't judge themselves harshly, and because of this, we do not feel judged by them. In fact, we feel that we are accepted by them just the way we are and we seek them out. At the same time, they set a high bar for us and in their presence we want to live up to it. In the presence of a Leader Coach with high self-esteem, the Talent is motivated to take risks and approach challenges with a positive attitude.

Healthy self-esteem rests on the principles of integrity, authenticity, and self-reliance discussed in the previous chapter. Living our values and striving for consistency in our every interaction gives us something to feel good about. It is hard to have a positive self-image when we know we are not living in alignment with those things that are most important to us.

To enhance our self-esteem, it is essential to assume full control of our lives (under the umbrella of whatever divine or spiritual power we believe in). When we let others control our lives, we are giving up the most important element of self-esteem: exercising our free will. This does not mean we cannot serve others. Quite the contrary. We may choose to be a servant, we do it with power because it is our choice and not one made for us.

Similarly, if we want to build self-esteem we must also reduce our dependency on others. The more we are dependent on others, the more we lower our self-esteem. This does not mean abandoning our relationships and communities; it means becoming a full partner in all our relationships. It means seeing service as a way of honoring others and using our gifts for others rather than being subservient. The great coach accepts that he does not have power over others, but he also recognizes that he is not powerless: he always has the power to serve others.

The beauty of self-esteem is that it liberates attention and energy from being bound up in the self and instead makes them available for others. The early twentieth-century psychologist Abraham Maslow recognized this in his famous "hierarchy of needs." His pyramid model, which is based on the principle that the lower-level needs must be fulfilled before we can turn to the higher ones, placed "esteem needs" as a prerequisite for "self-actualization needs" and "self-transcendence needs." Interestingly, the latter was not even included in his original version of the model, but was added in later life. It is particularly relevant for coaches, because true coaching is all about self-transcendence—putting aside one's own immediate needs—in service of the Talent. What Maslow's model reminds us is that in order to put ourselves aside in this way, we must first establish the foundation of healthy self-esteem and self-actualization—building our own character and pursuing our own aspirations for excellence.

## FROM SELF-AWARENESS TO SELF-ACCEPTANCE TO SELF-TRANSFORMATION

Healthy self-esteem does not mean being perfect. It does not preclude being wrong, not having the answers, or making mistakes, big and small. But those with a healthy foundation of respect for themselves are much more likely to have the confidence to own up to their shortcomings. Even at times when they do not feel good about themselves, they have the ability to put that aside in order to be a good coach. They are comfortable being fully themselves, and therefore, they have the confidence to say "I don't know" or "I made a mistake" and to take responsibility for the consequences. People with low self-esteem, on the other hand, are less able to admit when they don't know how to do something, and more likely to be afraid of making mistakes and cover them up when they occur.

Healthy self-esteem is not an absence of self-doubt, anxiety, or self-criticism. It is unlikely that we will ever entirely eliminate these insecurities from our lives, but as we learn to identify them and the situations that bring them out, we will become more knowledgeable about their origins. Our self-doubt is then lessened because our awareness enables us to be more conscious and intentional in our response. The great coach is well aware of her own reactions to insecurity and the situations that trigger it. She can see insecurity for what it is and not allow it to drive herself to behave in manipulative ways. She has the strength not to act on it at the expense of others and not to permit it to direct her behavior.

What gives great coaches the confidence to trust themselves is a deep self-awareness. The Buddhist teacher Sakyong Mipham writes, "With a healthy sense of self, we feel at ease . . . we're centered within a state of contentment. We're not too hard on ourselves; at the same time, we're wise to our own little tricks. We know how we get slippery. We know when we're trying to get away with something. We're comfortable looking at ourselves honestly."[23]

Wise and influential men and women know that human existence is defined by the inescapable fact that we each carry within us both light and darkness, and one of the challenges of life is to make sense of it all. Read almost any book on leadership and you will be encouraged to build a foundation of self-awareness. That's good advice. Knowing who you are is important, however, your real power comes from not just self-awareness but from self-acceptance. While having a positive self-image and healthy self-esteem is important, so is embracing the not-so-good parts of who you are. Attempting to eliminate or suppress those parts of ourselves that we may feel don't fit our current roles would be akin to a film editor cutting out any scene containing strife or pain from a movie. When we do this, we dilute our authentic selves and we lose our personal power.

I began this chapter with a quote from Dylan Thomas that bears repeating: "I hold a beast, an angel, and a madman in me and my enquiry is as to their working, and my problem is their subjugation and victory, downthrow and upheaval, and my effort is their self-expression."[24] Reflect on that for a moment. If you think you don't have a dark side, ask yourself the following questions, honestly. Are you sometimes quietly pleased when misfortune falls on someone who has hurt you? Are you a little bit jealous of a classmate's greater career success? Have you ever taken undeserved credit for someone else's good work? Spoken poorly about someone behind their back? Said something you knew was untrue? Said something hurtful in anger? Okay, so you are human as well.

Accepting your dark side does not mean you need to surrender to forces that impair your effectiveness as a leader or as a coach. And it is definitely not an excuse for bad behavior. Paradoxically, self-acceptance is the essential first step toward self-transformation. Those who are armed with profound self-knowledge and self-acceptance are able to readily capitalize on their natural strengths while lessening the potential negative impact in areas of vulnerability.

Personality traits have long been assumed to be stable over time, that is, they persist throughout our life and constitute our true nature. While this is to some extent true, an overly narrow interpretation may lead to the risky assumption that the fundamental aspects of our personalities are immutable and unchangeable and that our patterns of behavior are carved in stone. Self-awareness allows us to distinguish between our inner traits and characteristics and the outer patterns of behavior that other people see and judge us on. While the former may be an intrinsic part of who we are, the latter are more malleable. And in fact, science is now discovering that as we change our outer patterns of behavior, we do in fact influence our inner selves as well. The relationship between these two dimensions is perhaps one of the most fertile areas for self-discovery and growth.

When you incorporate new practices into your interactions with others, you can actually become a different person in the process. Here is the secret sauce—every time you do something intentionally, you create a tiny new trail of neurons in your brain. As you do it repetitively, the trail becomes a well-worn pathway. As it becomes a habit, it becomes a concrete freeway. It then becomes part of you. Your brain rewires itself.

Through this kind of self-awareness, you can take greater responsibility for changing those elements of your character that can be changed, and restraining those that cannot.

Coaching is a state of mind: it's about your belief in yourself and your trust that you will be able to handle whatever comes your way, no matter how unplanned or unexpected. It's being aware of your limitations and your strengths, accepting both, and doing your utmost to be responsible for them. It's about expecting the natural self-doubt that is the invisible companion of anyone who is attempting to accomplish great things and it's about not letting that self-doubt inhibit you. It's about daring to believe that something inside you is infinitely greater than the events of the day.

## SELF-APPRECIATION

Experience teaches us that everything in the coaching relationship begins with the coach. In chapter nine, we'll be talking about the principle of appreciation as a key element of the connection between coach and Talent. But the Leader Coach must first apply the principle of appreciation to him or herself. Authenticity depends on looking at everything and everyone, including oneself, through the same lens. To truly see another with an appreciative eye, one must be able to look at oneself the same way. It's difficult, if not impossible, to help someone else take a positive approach to themselves when one's own approach is not equally positive.

The habit of appreciation is a discipline the coach must keep. It means accepting and embracing our current successes and knowing our inherent worth. Even if each one of us is only a speck of dust in the universe, we know that we are each as uniquely gifted and wonderfully flawed as the most precious gemstone.

Appreciation also means being on the lookout for things we do well—in particular, the gifts and talents that are not the obvious ones that pop up on some strengths inventory. Often, there are talents we are avoiding, holding in exile. These gifts can be hard to find because they have rarely been used. Finding them and developing them can make them a source of inner strength and self-esteem.

Many of us structure our everyday, nonwork lives so that we rarely encounter the circumstances that will elicit the less visible and more neglected parts of our personalities. We lean toward the comfort of our well-known selves. On the other hand, the intensity and unpredictability of organizational life provides limitless opportunities for self-discovery. The wise leader recognizes this fertile ground for looking beyond easily recognized attributes, beyond those well-practiced behaviors that come naturally, to see the less expressed traits, those hidden and perhaps undiscovered dimensions of self.

How frequently and thoroughly do you study yourself? Do you make note of how you respond to conflict? How you make decisions? Consider how some of your traits may be situational.

Are they conspicuously absent in some situations? In what situations do you feel particularly potent, decisive and fully engaged? When do you feel weak and powerless? What makes you happy? Really sad? How can you use these insights to increase your effectiveness as a leader? We cannot view personality in black and white terms; it is much more accurately depicted as a spectrum of colors with varying hues and tints. The present day propensity to simplify personality theory into four letters or a handful of colors leads us to think of our traits in bipolar terms, that is, we are assumed to have one trait or its opposite. For example, you might see yourself as exclusively extroverted or introverted. The reality is, however, that personality traits occur along a continuum. Knowledge of where you naturally reside on that continuum and what causes you to slide from one end to the other is the key to your self-awareness and self-management.

While I've been advocating knowing both the light and the dark within yourself, it's important not to become overly preoccupied with your darker traits. Coaching is a challenging path that requires the power that comes from being firmly grounded in your strengths. One of the most frequent causes of leadership failure is not lack of ability, but rather the leader's preoccupation with his or her weaknesses. We all have flaws and shortcomings and our imperfections will always haunt us to some degree. Great coaches are able to be aware of, and manage, their weaker qualities. They honor their big mistakes and failures as life's lessons. However, they seize their power by focusing primarily on their many natural strengths and talents.

When we focus on our weaknesses, we tend to direct our thoughts toward the possibility of loss and failure and, in so doing, we move from power to powerlessness. We create cracks in the foundation of our character, and slowly, but surely, diminish our faith in our ability to succeed.

When we reach a place where we truly value and appreciate ourselves, the people around us instinctively know and respond to us more positively. We will feel comfortable bringing the whole of who we are into the coaching conversation and revealing ourselves. In this sense, self-esteem brings us back to authenticity—feeling appreciative of who we are allows us to be genuine in our interactions with others.

There is a multiplicity of rich threads woven into the complex fabric of our humanity. This is the brilliant tapestry at our core that defines our ethos, our essence. It is an amalgam of our experiences, characteristics, talents, strengths and weaknesses and a myriad of other aspects. When we are able to bring this entire tapestry to our work, we access our full reservoir of power. Great coaches not only draw much of their power by embracing who they really are, all their strengths and weaknesses. They also recognize that all of it is important because it constitutes their authentic self. There is no power greater than the freedom and stability of operating from an authentic platform, comfortable with who we are.

## A WORK IN PROGRESS

If you're someone with high standards, this appreciative embrace of your full self may be a significant challenge. You are likely your own worst critic. You may always feel as if you're falling short. Building healthy self-esteem means walking a fine line. On one hand, you must resist the unhelpful stance of perfectionism; yet on the other, you must be careful not to let yourself off the hook or lower your standards. The key to this balance is to see yourself as being on an adventure. The Talent is a work in progress and so are you. *You* today are different than the *You* who was on this planet yesterday. You are changing every day, even if in very small ways. Artists will often make numerous rough sketches of their paintings before putting brush to canvas. When we look at these sketches, we know they are simply preludes to the final masterpiece. We don't judge the sketch negatively because it is incomplete. We know that it is a work in progress. The same applies to each of us as coaches. No one assumes this role fully equipped for all its demands. At its most basic level, healthy self-esteem rests on understanding this fundamental truth about being human. We are all continuously evolving and changing, and need to recognize that this is a source of great strength.

A lack of self-acceptance undermines all aspects of our work—our focus, energy, learning and, ultimately, our enjoyment of the journey. Coaches gain great power when they accept their imperfections as inevitable and as opportunities for personal exploration and change. Anger can fuel action. Jealousy can evolve into admiration. Guilt, selfishness, greed and insensitivity can spur thoughtfulness about meaning in life. Our dark sides present opportunities to fully explore what it means to be human; to learn, grow and change and not stay hidden deep inside us as permanent personal deficits.

I have learned much from my friend and client, Michael Molinaro, Chief Learning Officer for New York Life, not the least of which is that all development, and especially leadership development, is a journey, not a destination. To make his point, he once told me that, "Great leaders do not really exist. Those we consider to be great leaders are deeply committed men and women who choose, every day, to get on the road toward great leadership. It is more of a vector than an end point." This perspective is invaluable for us as coaches as we seek ways to help the Talent shift onto new, more fruitful pathways.

Ultimately, we build self-esteem not from believing that we have arrived, but from our ability to keep moving while knowing that we always have further to go. The great coaches I know have their own challenging high performance development plans. They know that it is in working towards their own aspirations that they gain respect and appreciation for themselves.

To find the best in another individual, you must first have the capacity to find the best in yourself. To inspire others, you must first discover your own sources of inspiration. Nurture your passions and you will find the way to nurture the passions of others.

## HEALTHY SELF-ESTEEM VS. EGO

Healthy self-esteem is quite different from what we might call egotism, arrogance, or narcissism. It's not bragging, self-promotion, or over-confidence. In fact, those behaviors are often signs of the opposite trait: low self-esteem. People who spend excessive energy trying to convince others of their value and worth are often trying to conceal their perceived failings from public view. People who constantly relate their triumphs to everyone who will listen are sometimes hoping that if others believe they are successful, eventually they will too. Low self-esteem generally drives people to behave in ways that are far from coach-like.

Ego, in the vernacular sense of the term, tends to have a connotation of relativity to others. It says, "I am better than..." High self-esteem, on the other hand, doesn't rely on being better than anyone else. It is only about who you are. I believe it's possible to really like yourself and really like other people without making a judgment about who is better.

Interestingly, although those with high ego needs are always comparing themselves to others, they don't really have that much interest in others. They see others only as competitors or measuring sticks for their own success. The coach with healthy self-esteem, however, is not threatened by the successes of others. She revels in it.

Do you care about others? This is the basic price of entry to most helping vocations, but coaching requires more. Coaches don't simply help people get through a rough patch in life or solve a vexing problem. Coaches help others make real, sustained changes in their lives, and their ability to do this rests on their response to a very personal question. *Do you delight in the success of others?*

The master coach is able to be appreciative without comparison, and she is genuinely curious about other paths that are very different from her own. She is inspired by other people's achievements and uses the good feeling they generate to propel herself further along her own path.

When ego or arrogance is concealing a lack of self-esteem in the coach, the coaching conversation will inevitably be compromised. The coach may want to get credit for the success of the coaching, for example, or want the Talent to say positive things about him to others. He may need to feel like a superhero. As a result, he may make choices that lead to short-term wins rather than keeping the Talent's long-term interests in mind. He'll be hesitant to confront or raise uncomfortable questions for fear that the Talent won't like him or will speak poorly about him. He may even compromise his own values in order to make a positive impression. A coach who is naturally articulate and perceptive might fall into the trap of talking too much, offering her own solutions, when in fact the best thing might be to sit quietly and let the Talent come up with their own answers.

We can only know and relate to others as well (or as poorly) as we know and relate to ourselves. Shift the initial focus to yourself. Challenge yourself to gain the necessary self-appreciation to bring that authentic self—with all its imperfections—fully into the coaching relationship. This doesn't mean the conversation will be all about you. In fact, quite the opposite. When you can do this, you can hand the keys to the Talent, sit back, and enjoy the ride. This journey is not about you. And thankfully, you no longer need it to be.

## WHEN YOU LIKE YOURSELF, YOU DON'T NEED OTHERS TO LIKE YOU

The desire to be liked and admired by others is a natural human need. However, it can drive us to compromise our own integrity and authenticity in all kinds of ways. In the coaching relationship, it's particularly destructive and, if left unchecked, can be a significant obstacle to the kinds of conversations that are necessary for real progress. One of the reasons that healthy self-esteem is so important is that it frees the coach from the grip of this need. Of course, we all prefer that others think well of us, but if we fundamentally think well of ourselves and are striving for integrity, we can take the risk to not always be popular in the short term.

I advise anyone who aspires to be a great coach—or to be a leader in any arena of life—to stop being overly concerned about how they look to others and focus on living up to their own standards. I guarantee that, if created after deep reflection, those standards will be far higher than those set by others.

When I'm at my best, as a coach, my desire to be admired is subordinated. I won't say it never arises, but I've made a deal with myself that I'll let it go for the sake of the coaching process. I know that in our conversation, at some point I'm going to confront the Talent, and there's a very good chance that at least initially they will dislike me for it. They may thank me later, or they may not, and that's a risk I'm willing to take. Even the most deeply committed servant leader will not please everyone. The key is to stop trying to please people but instead seek ways to use our natural gifts to be of real service to them.

You can tell when someone has mastered coaching because they can put aside the need to be liked and admired and do exactly what they believe in their heart of hearts to be the best thing for the talent. In contrast, a coach who is constantly seeking the approval and admiration of others is clearly still a coach in training.

## THE POWER OF HUMILITY

Having spent these many pages extolling the virtues of self-esteem, I will now take a moment to dwell on an equally important quality of great coaches: humility. This may seem at first to contradict everything I've just said, but as the great Martin Luther King wisely said, "The strong man holds in a living blend strongly marked opposites. . . . The idealists are usually not realistic, and the realists are not usually idealistic. . . . Seldom are the humble self-assertive, or the self-assertive humble. But life at its best is a creative synthesis of opposites in fruitful harmony."[25]

In the master coach, that "creative synthesis of opposites" blends healthy self-esteem with genuine humility. She recognizes that no matter what levels she has achieved, she is not always right, she cannot have all the answers and she can and will make mistakes. Humility, sometimes confused with self-abasement, is in fact, quite the contrary. Humility elevates us and gives us power in many ways. Consider the amount of energy that we waste to keep our masks in place—the public disguises we wear to hide the fact that we are imperfect. When we shed pretense and false pride, when we act from a lack of self-importance, in short, when we practice the simple art of being humble, we release that energy to do great things.

"We come nearest to the great when we are great in humility,"[26] wrote the poet Rabindranath Tagore. When you read the biographies of the notable leaders and influential figures in history, two themes are often interwoven through the pages: a gratitude for the opportunity to serve others, and humility in the face of the challenges of leadership. We gain true and lasting power when we realize that, even though leaders are often in the spotlight, true leadership is about others, not about us.

How humbling, and at the same time ennobling, it is to approach our leadership from the point of view of what we can do for others rather than what we can do for ourselves. Much has been said about servant leadership, but it bears repeating. As Robert Greenleaf aptly put it long ago: ". . . it begins with the natural feeling that one wants to serve, to serve *first*."[27] When we focus on growing those we lead, we grow ourselves. When we focus on giving power to those we lead, we gain even greater power.

It is, however, not easy to consistently practice humility when you are blessed with being in a position of authority and enjoying the trappings of success, whether those look like an office with a door, a title of shift supervisor, or a chauffeur and private plane. The power associated with being a leader, at any level, can make us forget what a privilege it is. If we stop to think for a minute what that privilege entails, we would be in awe of our role in leading people. This responsibility should humble us.

Leadership is indeed a high calling. Leading people, having an impact on their careers and lives, is very special work and should be treated as such. When we view it this way, this attitude becomes ingrained in our daily routines, and people respond positively to this. People go the extra mile to support an unassuming leader who treats them with respect and dignity and, conversely, withhold their discretionary effort from the arrogant, self-important leader. Any time people withhold their best, the leader is weakened.

When leaders are genuinely grateful to have the opportunity to lead, others sense this and are more likely to welcome them as coaches. We do well to remember that a coach is only as powerful as the Talent permits. At any time, the coach can lose their support and thereby his role. A coach can be fired mid-sentence and never know they were fired. As with beauty, coaching is in the eye of the beholder. The coach who understands this will never be accused of arrogance.

Here is an important question for every coach to consider. In your relationships and conversations with those you coach, is there room enough for them? Or is most of the space occupied by you? People want to see the bigger version of themselves reflected in their coach's eyes; this precious image will not be there if the coach is the center of attention. With an arrogant coach, there is room only for the Talent's small self, not their big self. How do people feel about themselves when they are in your presence? We cannot set out to make everyone like us. We cannot control how people feel about us. But how we feel about ourselves has a huge impact on how people feel about themselves when they are in our presence. This is the discipline of the selfless Leader Coach. Genuine humility, coupled with healthy self-esteem, creates an environment in which, no matter what their differences in rank, both Talent and coach see themselves as equal in humanity.

# 8

# Noble Intention

*What nobility of feeling! To sacrifice your own pleasure
to preserve the comfort of others! It is a thing,
I confess, that would never occur to me.*

—SUSANNA CLARKE, *Jonathan Strange and Mr. Norrell*

Great coaching starts with self-sacrifice. The great coach chooses to temporarily subordinate his or her interests, needs, wants, and aspirations and instead, direct all the attention, space and energy to the Talent in order to advance their agenda. This is particularly difficult in Western cultures that are deeply invested in self-advancement, self-promotion, self-determination, self-everything. The great coach shifts the focus entirely to the Talent. I call this having "noble intention."

This may sound simple enough, but in reality, we can have many motives for coaching someone. A leader will almost certainly be driven by concerns about productivity, employee engagement, and so on. He might also have specific frustrations with a team member that he seeks to address through coaching, or organizational needs he hopes to meet by improving that person's performance. Some coaches may be seeking acknowledgment for being helpful, insightful, and caring. Others may simply enjoy the one-on-one engagement and the change of role. Many professional coaches do what they do because they get great personal satisfaction from knowing that their work is making an indelible, positive mark. All these are honorable motives, but the great coach is prepared to put all these aside if the coaching is to be truly powerful. The primary motive of the master coach is only this: to help the Talent unlock their abilities, triumph over their challenges, find their own solutions, and pursue their aspirations. True coaching is focused solely on the other person.

Even though the great coach needs to freely subordinate his motives for coaching an individual, he needs to be committed to the work at a deeply personal level. The burning desire to be a positive, creative force in the lives of others is an essential requirement for being a good coach. Coaching is a rewarding, yet often a difficult and arduous journey. Without this clear desire to coach, that journey can be devoid of pleasure. Great coaches possess not only the will to coach; they also have no doubt about their motives. They are clear that their reason for coaching is, above all, to catalyze growth and development in the Talent. This is the oil that fires their internal furnace—it's what fuels their power to be influential. It's easy to spot these coaches. There is an energy that radiates from them when they speak about their role. They feel bound to do their very best for the good of others.

Remember, the essence of the coaching perspective is that other people are full of potential. They are naturally talented, innately resourceful, and destined for greater things. They are also fully capable of making their own decisions, solving their own problems, and seizing their own opportunities, and are much more likely to follow through when they do. Noble intention is the expression of this perspective in action.

It takes a special person to focus on another's career and aspirations, but that's exactly what a great coach does. She does not feel the need to impress, nor does she even need to be told that her coaching was of significant value to the Talent. As discussed in the previous chapter, the best coaches have healthy self-esteem and a clear appreciation of their own gifts and talents. They don't need to feed their egos by showing the Talent how smart they are. This is noteworthy because all too often new coaches will subtly make the coaching about them, looking for the Talent to affirm their value as a coach. Seasoned coaches, on the other hand, have a quiet confidence in their own abilities that allows them to approach another with noble intention.

As coaches, the more we can remove ourselves from the agenda and pass it over to the Talent, the greater the impact the coaching relationship will have. That doesn't mean the coach takes no pleasure in the role he or she is playing, but that pleasure comes simply from knowing that he or she is making a difference, whether or not it is acknowledged or seen.

This noble intention is rare, but it is not out of reach for most of us. In fact, I believe there is something deep within each human being that, given the right circumstances, wants to do good in the lives and development of others. The irony of the coaching role, however, is that when coaches are at their very best, and the coaching process is producing outstanding results, the Talent should be the one getting the credit. The test of noble intention is that the coach is unconcerned with the lack of recognition, because he or she is not in it for the glory or the praise.

## THE COACH DOESN'T ALWAYS KNOW BEST

Many people approach the coaching process with the assumption that they have knowledge, tools, and insights that will be valuable to others, and that they likely have greater capacities to solve problems and make decisions than those they will be coaching. This may be true. But even if it is, to become a great coach, one needs to move beyond this assumption.

The organizational consultant Jut Meininger wisely wrote, "The best answers to many of our most perplexing problems are often already tucked away in the far recesses of our own heads! We sometimes have trouble getting to them, and then, typically, we go around asking others for help. Very often what we are looking for (even if we cannot express it in so many words) is not advice, but help in thinking the problem through for ourselves. Advice-giving, in fact, often undercuts this process."[28]

The master coach has grasped this little-known truth, and knows that his job is to help the talent access those far recesses and find the answers for themselves. In fact, one of the distinguishing characteristics of the master coach is that she always works toward creating self-reliance in the Talent, rather than making the Talent dependent on her.

This is not to say the coach should withhold any resources he has to offer. He approaches the Talent with hands open and full, offering time, knowledge, experience, even connections. But these never take the place of helping the Talent find access to the untapped resources within themselves.

Noble intention requires that you take a backseat, or at least a passenger seat, and throw the keys to the Talent. "Here, why don't you drive?" You may know you're a good driver, perhaps even a better driver, but you're not driving now. Someone else is, and it's in their best interests to take the wheel and learn for themselves. Can you relax enough to enjoy the freedom of watching the Talent do the driving? You're looking down the road together, not knowing where the next turn will take you, but your hands are off the steering wheel. You might suggest directions when asked, or alert the Talent to a danger they cannot see, but you do not take over the driving. You have the privilege of sharing the journey, but you cannot direct it, nor can you determine its destination. This is not your journey. In fact, when you come to the humbling realization that you have no idea which destination is best for the Talent, you will have achieved the zenith of the coach's role.

## HOW HIGH CAN YOU COACH?

Here's an important question for the coach to consider: Can you coach someone to a higher level of performance than you have achieved yourself? Or do you, perhaps unintentionally, subject others to your own limitations? How high can you really coach? The reason this question matters is that it can shine a light on the coach's sometimes unconscious attitudes in relationship to the Talent. Unless the coach has done the hard work of gaining self-awareness, building healthy self-esteem, and forging noble intention, it is likely that to some extent he or she may still feel threatened by the accomplishments and success of others.

To coach beyond your own level requires an unusual degree of self-mastery. Most of us can readily coach others to succeed when it's clear they are working on performance issues that we have mastered. However, to coach for performance beyond our own achievements, we need to exercise discipline. We must work hard to ensure that our focus remains on the Talent's potential and that we do not sabotage their efforts by projecting our own fears and self-imposed limitations onto them.

This challenge is magnified for the coach who is also a manager or leader. These people are not just threatened existentially by the idea of coaching someone to surpass them—it could quite literally be true. A manager could be coaching the person who will one day replace him. A team leader could be coaching someone with whom she may end up competing for a promotion. Yet to coach effectively, these leaders will have to have the courage and self-discipline to put their fears aside. And they will have to do so convincingly, so that the Talent truly experiences that absence of rank and self-concern in their coaching.

Sadly, this is rare. I often hear organization leaders attribute much of their success to hiring people who are smarter than they are. This may be true, but I see little evidence of these same leaders encouraging their team members to outperform them. I seldom, if ever, hear these leaders talking about how they can help the best and the brightest in their organizations pass them on their way up the leadership hierarchy. It's been my observation that most of us are naturally inclined to coach others up to our own level of performance, but not beyond. It's not that we consciously keep others down but rather that we have that all-too-human tendency to see ourselves as the target to which our team members should aspire.

It is human nature to project not only our own beliefs about what's possible but also our own fears about the risks involved in performing at a higher level onto other people. As a coach, you need to ask yourself: "Am I prepared for the Talent to succeed beyond anything I have imagined or thought possible?" If you can answer with a resounding "yes!" then you are likely approaching the role with noble intention.

The master coach doesn't try to make the Talent more like himself. He tries to help them become the very best version of themselves. The very best coaches take themselves and their position right out of the conversation, and this is a reflection of their character development and integrity. To see a level of greatness in others that is not measured against one's own achievements and to coach others towards it requires the noblest of intention.

There is a final element to the quality of noble intention, which again, is particularly challenging for the coach. Can you be unattached to the outcome of the coaching work? For an external executive coach, this is relatively easy. When I work inside a client organization, I am not deeply invested in what the Talent decides to focus on and what they do or do not do. My only job is to help them to live up to their own highest standards. For example, if those standards require them to spend more time with their family than at the office, I can happily coach them to attend to those most important values. However, for a manager within an organization, that would be more of a challenge. By nature of her position, she is attached to the Talent's performance. Her results are based on how others perform. For her, it is a much greater challenge to remain detached from the outcome of the coaching conversation, even if it has a negative impact on her role in the organization. And yet for her to be an effective coach, it is necessary that she do so.

# A MEETING OF MINDS

Noble intention is both a mental and emotional discipline. It is not something that simply materializes. It requires taking deliberate, considered steps to ensure that the interests of the Talent are of primary concern at all times. The coach puts on the attitude of noble intention like she puts on clothes each day. She prepares herself for each encounter, whether formal or informal, rather than leaving the meeting of two minds to chance. A coach who has noble intention has made a conscious decision to see the Talent with appreciative eyes in order to unleash their potential, even if it means temporarily sacrificing her own needs.

How will the Talent know that the coach has noble intention? What will it look like from their side? They will look forward to their time with you. They will see you as someone who believes in them, someone who sees their unrealized potential. They will see you as a person of stature who looks beyond the here and now, who wants others to see their own exciting new possibilities. When they meet with you, they will sense that you are there for them. They will feel well respected and well regarded by you, no matter what. They will appreciate your thoughtful questions and the way you listen with intent and engage their responses. They will feel comfortable sharing their dreams and fears, and their successes and failures, with you. In effect, they will grant you the right to be their coach.

Interestingly, it is quite normal for the Talent to be a bit apprehensive when starting to work with a great coach. They will dislike you when you voice challenging ideas and perspectives. They will be frustrated with you when you have no answers for them. They will be angered at your direct, unvarnished feedback. However, if you have truly acted with noble intention; some part of them, the part that looks for real value, will hear the message, perhaps only recognizing the truth in it at a later time.

When I look back on my own career, I can see now that my best coaches did not view me as a problem to be fixed or even a person to be transformed for the betterment of the organization. Rather, they were people motivated by the opportunity to facilitate my personal and professional growth. I assume that they found considerable meaning and reward within our relationship. They became excited about seeing me reach my own potential—a level of success they knew was possible even when I failed to see it myself. Having recognized and accepted their own abilities, these men and women were able to put aside their needs in order to focus everything they had on my development. In those coaching moments, they offered all their gifts and talents to serve me. Because they did so, their impact on my career and my life will never be forgotten.

## THE MOST IMPORTANT WORK IN THE WORLD?

All this being said, it might seem that the role of coach is rather an austere and self-sacrificing calling, devoid of satisfaction or reward. It is indeed a bumpy and often solitary trail. As Ron Crossland and Boyd Clarke said: "Some will judge you unfairly, blaming you for their lack of success. Others will expect resources you cannot give, answers that you do not have, and permission you cannot grant. You will be misquoted. Your judgment will be questioned. You will certainly stumble. Failure will stalk you like a predator."[29] Along the way you will receive a lot of feedback, both good and bad. There will be few moments of gratitude and great personal sacrifices.

I believe there are few roles in life that are more rewarding than coaching. It is just that these rewards come more as serendipitous byproducts rather than items that drive or shape the agenda. Great coaches recognize that the overarching value of being a catalyst for the learning and development of others needs to take temporary precedence over actively seeking their own rewards. But make no mistake, those rewards will come, if you are patient.

Several years ago, one of my fellow coaches came to speak to me. So inspired was he by the breakthroughs his client had made in their work and leadership, he almost did cartwheels into my office. "Gregg," he exclaimed, "I am convinced that our work is the most important in the world!" I wanted to affirm his enthusiasm, but also felt it was my duty to put his statement in context. So I gently reminded him that there are many people out there doing people-focused work that is much more significant than ours, including surgeons, politicians, social activists, medical researchers, entrepreneurs, and so on.

Undeterred, he replied, "Gregg, I know. But I work with those people and I help them do extraordinary things." His statement gave me pause. It inspired me to reflect more deeply on the power of coaching. We may very well be the butterfly who causes a hurricane. We never know where our impact will spread and we may never see its results directly. People often tell me that they expected coaching to help them at work. What they didn't expect was for it to help them in life. And yet because of the coaching experience, they find that they've become not just a better performer in the office, but a better parent, a better partner, a better neighbor, a better member of the community.

These days, many people advertise themselves as "life coaches." I confess that I, like many of my colleagues who are also leadership coaches, am sometimes a bit skeptical about the practices of those who wear this mantle. When I first heard an early coaching instructor exhort the class to "coach the whole person," I rolled my eyes, thinking to myself, "These poor souls have no appreciation for the power of having a laser-like focus on a critical competency like leadership." I could not have been more wrong. Many years and hundreds of clients later, I have learned that even if the starting issue is a narrow and well-defined business challenge, the person I am coaching brings their entire self into the conversation. To serve them well, I need to be willing and able to coach the entire person. It doesn't matter if you are a leadership coach, a parenting coach, a career coach, a relationship coach—you still have a whole person in front of you with all their wonderfully complex beliefs, characteristics and aspirations.

If I'm lucky, I hear about the results of my work, but more often, my satisfaction, my sense of accomplishment, needs to emanate from my own belief in the long-term power of coaching. That doesn't make it less significant. In a sense, my colleague was right. I might not choose quite the terms he used, but I can never underestimate the significance of unleashing human potential in any one individual. We cannot know where that newly released energy and talent will go, and how many people it will affect. What we can know, as coaches, is that we've done our very best to have an indelible, positive impact on people who will then touch the lives of others. What more important work could there be than this?

# 9

# Emotional Intelligence

*Let's not forget that the little emotions are the great captains of our lives and we obey them without realizing it.*
—VINCENT VAN GOGH, Letter to Theo, 1889

When it comes to the character of the coach, there is one final dimension that must not be neglected: emotional intelligence. Put simply, emotional intelligence is about learning to recognize our own feelings and those of others and to manage these feelings well in ourselves and in our relationships. And these abilities are central to the building of character. In fact, Daniel Goleman, who popularized the notion with his bestselling book, has said that character is simply "an old-fashioned word for the body of skills that emotional intelligence represents."[30]

Before I go any further, let me just acknowledge that many people, myself included, instinctively cringe when words like "emotion" get mixed up with business. We've been trained to see our workplaces as domains where rationality reigns, and messy, touchy-feely things like emotions are best left at home. (I find it amusingly ironic that this instinctive antipathy to emotions is itself an emotional response, triggered in the brain by a lifetime's habit, and having little to do with the rational, conscious, smart aspects of the self . . . but I digress.) Thankfully, over time, my perspective on emotions has far outgrown my old-fashioned and not-so-rational desire to segregate them from the world of work. And I'm not alone. Today, more enlightened business-people across the world recognize that it's neither possible nor desirable to leave our emotions out of business. As Dan Shapiro writes in *Harvard Business Review,* "First, it's hard to pull off, as anyone who has had sweaty palms or a pounding heart during a heated conversation can attest. Second, and more important, it's not in your interest to do so."[31]

Wise leaders and great coaches accept that there is emotion in every human endeavor—business, family, sports, and politics—and it affects everyone. Sometimes those emotions have positive effects. They bind relationships with warmth and vitality, infusing projects with passion, inspiring loyalty, and motivating teams. Other times, they have negative consequences—clouding judgment, delaying decisions, and leading to conflict and drama. But they cannot be avoided, especially by those who aspire to lead.

Emotions can be a close ally or a strong opponent, depending on how conscious you are of their triggers, habitual manifestations, and impact. They are portals of self-discovery if we choose to make them so. Nowhere does the adage that "knowledge is power" apply more aptly than in the case of knowledge of one's emotions. In my experience, there are three things that are important to know about emotions: emotions are connected to things that matter to us; they provide us with very useful information; and, the drive to experience or not experience an emotion determines a lot of our behavior. This makes emotions one of the most powerful forces within us. As such, they are an essential and unavoidable part of coaching.

Emotions are frequently referred to as energy in motion. This is an apt description, as one of the formal definitions of energy is "the potential for causing changes" and emotions definitely precipitate significant changes in our behavior. To get a sense of the power of emotions, think of the feelings that spur terrorism and war, on the one hand, and heroic acts of bravery or major movements in art, on the other hand. On a physical level, think about how the emotion of fear can bring about physiological changes such as a pounding heart, or how anger can constrict our vocal chords, how embarrassment makes us blush, and how gratitude can make our face break into a smile. All these changes are different forms of energy with different effects, positive or negative.

Emotions are critical to leadership. In my estimation, leaders today rarely fail because they back the wrong product or make a misstep in an acquisition. They fail because they are insensitive, critical, selfish, arrogant, or negative. In other words, *they fail because they are emotionally weak.* They fail because they are unable or unwilling to harness the power of their own emotions and those of others. Research supports this observation. The respected Center for Creative Leadership (CCL), which works with leaders from more than 2,000 organizations, including most of the Fortune 100 companies, found that the primary causes of career derailment involve deficiencies in emotional competence, specifically difficulty in handling change, inability to work well in a team, and poor interpersonal relations.[32]

It is through observing this repeatedly that I have come to believe that the single most powerful force in the domains of both leadership and coaching is emotion. As uncertain and unpredictable as this is, it is very important for us, as coaches, to understand that this one single factor influences all our work.

Emotion is defined in most dictionaries as a mental state or a rapid-response feeling that arises spontaneously rather than through a conscious effort. A narrow interpretation of this definition would suggest that emotions are totally beyond our control. In fact we do have considerable power: the power to be intentional about our use of emotion, to decide when to let an emotion flow, unrestrained, and when to re-channel its course. This brings us back to the critical issue of self-mastery.

The emphasis on rationality and order in our workplaces tends to marginalize and devalue emotions, and therefore many leaders are unprepared for the extensive amount of energy and effort that is required to keep emotions in check. But emotional intelligence is not only about controlling and repressing feeling. It is also the understanding that the more we acknowledge and honor our emotions, expressing them authentically and intentionally, the more power we have to lead. Imagine yourself as a leader who readily displays potent emotional states such as intense enthusiasm, keen interest, unbridled curiosity, sheer exuberance, victory, great passion, joy, hope, optimism, pride and gratitude. Surely these are what Bertrand Russell must have had in mind when he talked of "creative emotions from which a good life springs."

Think about how potent these states make us feel: how energized we are in their grip; how we are filled with possibility when we experience them. Think of athletes who achieve excellence in their sport; consider the fervency, excitement, and intensity that they experience; their unwavering optimism and anticipation of winning. Could athletes perform at their best, devoid of emotion? So it is with leaders. Goleman borrows a term from the psychologist Mihaly Csikszentmihalyi to succinctly capture this state: Flow. "Being able to enter flow is emotional intelligence at its best; flow represents perhaps the ultimate in harnessing the emotions in the service of performance and learning. In flow the emotions are not just contained and channeled, but positive, energized, and aligned with the task at hand."[33]

The leader as coach will be infinitely more effective in serving the Talent if she is in that state of flow—free and at ease with her own emotions.

## BECOMING EMOTIONALLY INTELLIGENT

The idea of emotional intelligence emerged during the mid-twentieth century, but it wasn't until the nineties that it caught on, thanks to Goleman's popular book and his application of the idea to business. A psychologist and former *New York Times* correspondent, Goleman stumbled upon an academic article on the topic by John Mayer and Peter Salovey, and became, in his words, "electrified by the notion."[34]

Goleman identified five domains of emotional intelligence: self-awareness, motivation, self-regulation, empathy, and adeptness in relationships.[35] In his research at nearly two hundred large, global companies, he found that truly effective leaders are distinguished by high levels of each of these traits, which add up to a high degree of emotional intelligence. "It's not that IQ and technical skills are irrelevant," he wrote in his seminal 1998 Harvard Business Review article, "They do matter, but . . . they are the entry-level requirements for executive positions. My research, along with other recent studies, clearly shows that emotional intelligence is the sine qua non of leadership. Without it, a person can have the best training in the world, an incisive, analytical mind, and an endless supply of smart ideas, but he still won't make a great leader."[36]

We're all born with plenty of emotions, but emotional intelligence is something we must develop over time, as we mature. It doesn't necessarily come naturally. In fact, by nature, we are quite the opposite—impulsive, superficial, self-absorbed, and lacking in self-knowledge. To become emotionally intelligent and powerful takes a real concerted effort, but it can be done. When one simply decides to study and master one's emotions, connect with and positively influence others, it's like turning on a light switch. The change is immediate. Overnight your leadership power and your coaching effectiveness will increase tenfold. It is remarkably straightforward and doable.

Here are four things I recommend for developing your emotional intelligence:

**1. Get up close and real personal with the real you.** Recognize and embrace your emotions. These are not simply outcroppings of your personality. Emotions are you. Think of spending your life swimming in a pool of your emotions. They are everywhere, and you are always under the influence of at least one of them. While you may think you know yourself well, most of us really don't.

Knowing your MBTI personality type is not enough. Step back to get some perspective and observe yourself carefully. Get up on your own balcony, as leadership authors Ronald Abadian Heifetz and Martin Linsky put it in their book *The Practice of Adaptive Leadership*. What really makes you tick? What makes you happy, sad, glad, and mad? Watch yourself interact with others. Become aware of your emotions as they occur. Note the events that trigger significant emotional reactions. Many of your historical emotional patterns are stored in an almond-shaped part of your brain called the amygdala. These can be changed but it takes lots of introspection and hard work.

Self-awareness is the first of Goleman's emotional intelligence skills, and that is appropriate, because it's foundational. It means being aware when an emotion surfaces and then being able to correctly identify the emotion. It's difficult to react properly to an emotion that we can't describe, so without developing self-awareness, you can't self-regulate, let alone interact skillfully with others. There are hundreds of emotions but most people can name less than a couple dozen. While we all understand the primary emotions such as joy, excitement, anger, and fear, many of us lack the emotional literacy to correctly identify the secondary ones, such as being mildly hurt or upset, feeling somewhat tense or worried, dealing with vague doubts and undefined confusions, being slightly skeptical and a little overwhelmed, feeling non-specific franticness and unexplained stress or anxiety. And yet, most of us live in that terrain, it seems, for at least some part of our careers. It is these minor emotional states that most often are our biggest energy drains, the culprits that can derail us from the achievement of our goals. It behooves us to raise our self-awareness of the less dramatic emotions and develop an action plan to understand their sources and to deal with them.

Being intelligent about our emotions also means being aware of the subtle nuances of various emotions. Armed with that information, we can make appropriate behavioral decisions. For example, anger can have many flavors: it can lean toward bitterness, resentment, frustration, or dislike, to name just a few variations. Narrowing down the specific flavor goes a long way toward being able to understand the reasons behind the emotions and make intelligent decisions about how to respond to the situation so that we don't drain our power. So it is with joy as well, to use another example. Let's say you're feeling an eager, happy glow as you contemplate adopting a certain path. It's important to know whether that feeling is just the excitement of the new, the relief at avoiding a more challenging but perhaps more appropriate course of action, or a genuine thrill and exhilaration stemming from the tangible, real benefits of the new path we are undertaking. These nuances can add valuable information to our decision-making processes.

In our exploration of emotions, we also need to be cognizant that the manifestation of one emotion can be a powerful clue to us about the absence of another emotion or state, as emotions tend to work in polarities. For example, an easy access to frustration or anger on daily issues can signal an absence of compassion. Feeling bored can be a sign of not being engaged and inspired by what we do. Feeling discouraged alerts us to the fact that we are not motivated. Being envious can be a signal that we lack self-confidence. We can use the awareness of these emotions as tools to discover what simmers beneath the surface of these intense feelings.

Finally, even the most phlegmatic among us have emotional hot buttons—once pressed, these trigger automatic reactions that can rob us of our self-control and leadership power. Those who have very young children know exactly what I mean. Your children are experts at pressing the buttons because they know exactly where they are. As a coach, you need to be aware of your buttons because the Talent may push them, unintentionally. Your self-knowledge will help you stay calm and centered even if an emotional storm has just been triggered, and keep your focus where it belongs: on the Talent.

**2. Become the master of your own emotional ship.** Stop being ruled by old patterns of feeling-thinking-acting that no longer serve you well. Get into the habit of pausing and reflecting. Ask yourself, "What's really happening here? Regardless of how I feel, what's the next best step for me, as a leader, to take?" In neuroscience terms, this means, give your neocortex a chance. This is the "I" part of you that resides in the upper part of your brain. It is the smart, cognitive part where you make rational, informed decisions. Don't leave the amygdala on its own or you will end up with the same old reactions. Introduce your neocortex to your amygdala. Get them talking. This will allow you to create the habit of fully experiencing your emotions while consciously selecting your reactions. This will be the main source of your leadership power.

**3. Practice empathy.** Empathy is one of the most essential emotional intelligence skills for the coach. Put simply, it is the ability to understand and share the feelings of another. And it's the "share" part that distinguishes empathy from its easier-to-achieve cousin, sympathy. Sympathy could be described as "feeling for" someone, but empathy is the capacity to "feel with" another person—to share or recognize emotions experienced by others. Dr. Brene Brown highlights this distinction beautifully: "Empathy is a vulnerable choice," she explains, "because in order to connect with you I have to connect with something in myself that knows that feeling."[37]

A formal definition of empathy is the ability to identify and understand another's situation, feelings and motives. It's our capacity to recognize and vicariously experience the concerns and issues others are facing. Common metaphorical language for empathy includes putting yourself in the other person's shoes, or seeing things through someone else's eyes. First Nations people have a beautiful way of expressing empathy as "walking a mile in someone else's moccasins." Moccasins are a symbol of the strength of Native North American people and this gives an even more profound interpretation of empathy as the ability to understand the struggles and challenges others face and the fortitude it requires to endure these challenges and stay the course.

Think about what this means for you as a coach. Can you really put yourself so deeply into the mind of the Talent that you can actually experience their feelings? So often, we confine our attention solely to our personal concerns and to the interests of a few people who are close to us. This tendency holds us captive in a narrow enclave from which it is impossible to truly expand our power, our capacity to affect others in a way that has substance and significance. No matter how accomplished we are, no matter how many skills, talents, and achievements we can claim as ours, no matter how wide our personal influence, it is all ultimately hollow if it does not include empathy for those who surround us.

Practice seeing the world through the eyes of others. Practice being totally present with others, even for a short time. Great coaches invest considerable time and energy in understanding others and seeking ways to serve them. Others are not simply pawns in their game but real people with unique needs, fears, aspirations, and, yes, their own amygdalae! Speaking of amygdalae, these little items make being truly empathetic quite difficult. We naturally see people through our own emotional patterns, which are formed from our experiences, values, and beliefs, and it takes a concerted effort to tune out the amygdala for a little while to really see others as they see themselves. Great coaches gain tremendous personal power by making this effort. Mediocre ones don't.

Empathy is essential for the master coach because it allows us to have a deeper connection with people who enter our lives; a genuine link moving from a surface association to a deeper, person-to-person relationship. This kind of connection involves seeing people in a way that can only come from a genuine concern for their welfare and success—seeing them in ways that they may have not seen themselves. Picasso once said: "I see for others in order to put on canvas the sudden apparitions which come to me." The coach who has this deep-seated empathy develops these kinds of eyes—ones that move away from self-focus to focusing on the other and, in the moment, seeing the very best that is at the core of that person and reflecting it back to the individual. This coach sees the spark of greatness, the vast potential that dwells in the person and is waiting to be released. Deep empathy doesn't stop with sharing people's fears and insecurities—it sees past those self-imposed limitations and barriers. And a core element of this kind of empathy is its lack of judgment. Empathy peels labels off people, and truly sees them as fellow humans. I like to think of it as seeing with the heart.

This type of empathy also means having a heightened awareness of when we begin to have stagnant impressions of people, impressions formed based on a first meeting or on a past incident. It's ensuring that our opinion about a particular person is not fossilized but, instead, continues to evolve to allow for subsequent positive impressions to alter original ones.

Empathy also involves realizing that we are echoes of those around us, those through whom we accomplish so much in our individual journey. It means not losing sight of how much of our success is dependent on other people's efforts, contributions, and talents. Empathy is the understanding and honoring of the role others play and connecting our personal power to them, as a conduit for them to realize their own aspirations and dreams. It's having the willingness, and making the allowance of time, to look into people's hearts so as to glean what these aspirations are. It's truly feeling these aspirations and realizing that they are no less intense and no less important than our own aspirations. But it doesn't stop there. It's about opening the portals for the expression and realization of these aspirations; it's about providing the opportunities for people to realize their own potential for greatness.

In *Creating the Good Life: Applying Aristotle's Wisdom to Find Meaning and Happiness*, James O'Toole talks about this worthy intention: "If Aristotle is right that the good life depends on developing one's human potential, then providing the conditions in which employees can do so is a clear moral responsibility of leaders of work organizations. The logic is inescapable: organizations that deny employees the chance to develop their potential deny them the opportunity to develop their humanity."[38]

How do we help others realize their full potential? We do so by believing in them, in their potential for greatness; by helping them discover their gifts and expand their abilities; by challenging them and by acknowledging them for what they try to create of themselves. We also help them make the connection between who they are today and the vision of who they can be. And we go out of our way to use our own power to make that vision come alive.

Truly developing empathy as a fundamental character attribute is a lifetime's journey that the master coach undertakes. As empathy matures, it becomes less of an effort-driven skill and more of a way of being. It's a decentering of the self and the development of a powerful sensitivity to others' feelings, actions, attitudes, and needs. The development of empathy is one of the noblest actions and most valuable we can undertake as coaches and as human beings.

**4. Stop sucking the light out of the room.** Are you a pervasive, positive influence on the people in your organization? When you walk into a room, does it become brighter or do you suck out all the light? Moods make all the difference. (Yes, you can choose your mood. When your neo-cortex and amygdala are on good speaking terms, you can engage that part of you that smiles, sees the best in others, is joyful and is nice to be around.) A coach's mood is especially infectious because of the nature of the coaching relationship. Great coaches have a contagious optimism about the future and constantly convey a strong sense of confidence in themselves and in the Talent. They bring light into every room they enter.

# HANDLING NEGATIVE EMOTIONS:
# IT IS OK TO GET ANGRY AT THE TALENT

How does the master coach handle the so-called negative emotions, like fear, anger, envy, greed, and jealousy? Conventional wisdom would dictate that these need to be controlled or even shunned; however, we cannot select which emotions we will experience just as one would select a new shirt. Negative emotions are a natural part of who we are; they are a part of our emotional framework. While most of us aim to be in a positive state of mind all the time, the reality is that negative emotions encroach upon us whether we like it or not. The aim, then, is to move away from the positive/negative dichotomy and to view all emotions as part of our overall emotional make up—to be present to the negative emotions without personal recrimination and to view them instead as messengers, carriers of important information about ourselves or other people, imparting precious, personal data that can either fuel our power or rob us of it, like energy bandits.

So what should you do if something the Talent says or does makes you angry? First, recognize that this is a good source of information, either about you, the Talent or, most likely, both. Have some important values been violated? Have you been disrespected? Did the Talent dishonor the coaching relationship? You need to be guided by one question: Will my response be helpful to the Talent or am I simply allowing my anger to form my reaction?

What makes all the difference is what we do with the information embedded in the emotions. Negative emotions are simply a signal to us that there is something that we are not able to handle in the moment. If we ignore the message, we start an energy leak. If, however, we take the time to become aware of what we are feeling, in the moment, and acknowledge the emotion, we are then able to use that intelligence to effectively deal with whatever is causing the negative emotion. People who have learned to function in their power, those who are highly attuned self-scientists, have trained themselves to address the small drop-lets before they become a flood. Everyone experiences these primordial emotions, at one time or other, but people who function in their power, who are emotionally competent, embrace these as inevitable learning opportunities and are not immobilized by them. Just as in the Third Law of Thermodynamics where heat seeks out cold, these individuals have learned, through experience, that the largest supply of energy will be diverted to the negative emotions if we let it, depleting the fuel needed for higher thoughts and higher states of emotions. Instead, they will identify the true cause of these emotions and resolve to address the source rather than let the emotions carry the day.

This brings us to another key point. We need to be able to have access to the full range of our emotions. This gives us the opportunity to play with a full deck of cards. It makes us nimble and flexible enough to react to widely varied situations, and to adapt as necessary, to different environments. Emotions color and enrich our interactions and experiences. If we have a limited range of emotions that we draw upon, we end up with a lot less coloring. For example, reining in love and joy can also block empathy and compassion. And the same wall we build to keep negative emotions out can also prevent positive emotions from entering. Think about how much we would miss if we didn't experience some of these emotional states, for example: boldness, elation, respect, delight, dynamism, passion, remorse, impatience, sadness and being appalled? Like an accomplished artisan, we need the full range of tools to function at our highest power, remembering that all emotions propel to action, even uncomfortable ones.

The master coach is not a machine devoid of feelings, flaws, and personality. When we withhold our uniqueness, we deprive the Talent of a rich source of information and insights. It is one of the central dilemmas of coaching that even though the coaching conversation is all about the Talent, the coach must bring all that he is into the coaching conversation, including her feelings, needs, fears, and aspirations. However, he must do so without allowing his issues to become an impediment to the learning of the Talent.

The master coach needs to be emotionally mature enough to not only deal with his own uncomfortable emotions, but those of the Talent as well. He must be strong enough to reject the Talent's request for sympathy, to not condone poor behavior, and to let the Talent suffer through changes, dilemmas, and uncertainty. He needs to have the courage to pursue profoundly difficult, emotion-laden topics; confront the Talent with their own irresponsibility; and identify reality in the face of strong denials from the Talent. Throughout the coaching process, he must be resilient enough to feel the emotional spikes that accompany the distress, anxiety, and other negative emotions that are experienced by the Talent.

## FEAR AND COURAGE: THE COACH'S COMPANIONS

The richest pathway in coaching is often the scariest. This may not be what you want to hear, but it's a truth I must share: fear is the constant companion of the coach. To coach is to act in spite of this fear. Your fears will change over the course of your career but they will stalk you relentlessly. I suspect that the four fears that most frequently haunt coaches are failure, rejection, humiliation, and the unknown. Our challenge is to act in the face of these fears. There cannot be genuine power without courage— the courage to act. Think about past events in your career or life journey where you opted not to seize an opportunity because of fear. How does this feel now? Seeing it from today's perspective, were your fears justified? Now switch tapes and play a different movie: see yourself seizing that very same opportunity with your consciousness today. How are you doing? Is the fear diminished? Is it even there? How often have we had fears in the past that we have overcome? Think of the first time you rode a bike or the first time you spoke in public.

The master coach seeks to summon up the courage to step up and function at her highest potential, every day, at every opportunity that presents itself. This requires courage—the courage to believe in her own personal giftedness, in her ability to express this giftedness in the moment, being receptive to any possibilities that come her way. "Courage," as Arthur Koestler put it, "is never to let your actions be influenced by your fears."

Here is a paradox: fear is an emotional asset, if we see it as a messenger of important information. It tells us that what we are afraid of must be challenging and risky for us; if not, we would not fear it. And inner strength comes from having the courage to face those challenges and risks and making a commitment to not let the fear stand in the way of achievement, in the way of reaching our highest potentiality. If we befriend fear, it becomes adrenaline for the soul. It gives us the energy and the exhilaration of action, it gives us courage. And courage, once committed to, creates an enormous internal reservoir of strength. It's common to believe that being courageous is synonymous with having no fears, while the opposite is true: having courage is acting despite our fears. It is going after precisely that which we are afraid to do. As Eleanor Roosevelt put it, courage is "looking fear in the face."

It's worth noting that fear is a companion of all leaders, at any level of the corporate hierarchy. It does not vanish in the senior leadership ranks. Rather, fears mutate in accordance with the increasing personal challenges that come with the territory and the more practice leaders get in taming their fears, the more courageous they become. Seasoned leaders use fear to their advantage; that is, they let it fuel their courage. They feel the fear but stay, nonetheless, steadfast to their purpose; they have developed a stoutness of mind and will to forge ahead at steady speed toward the achievement of their goals, relegating fear to the back seat. General Patton said: "Courage is fear holding on a minute longer."

Are there issues right now in your life where, no matter how challenging or discouraging they are, holding on longer would make a difference? How might a courageous outlook fortify your resilience and expand your repertoire of coping mechanisms?

What exactly is courage in a coach? It is that quality of mind or spirit that enables you to face change, risk and the unknown with self-possession, confidence and resolution. It suggests an inner strength on which you can draw when in difficult and challenging times. It is synonymous with mettle, which the dictionary defines as that capacity to rise to the challenge. It is resolution to pursue your purpose against all odds. Courage is doing the unpopular when you know it is the right thing to do. It is being petrified with fear but acting anyway. What is your personal definition of courage? If you practiced courage every day, at every opportunity, at every meeting, in every conversation, in all your internal dialogue, what would this be like? What image of you emerges? What would happen if you intentionally made several courageous decisions next week?

There is an element of exhilarating energy when we choose to practice courage. It gives us vitality and vigor. It pushes us, propels us forward. It gives us permission to use all our talents and it sometimes even surprises us with a showing of talents and strengths that we were unaware we possessed. Acting courageously opens up an unexplored storage of personal gifts. Which unopened gifts do you think you might find in your repertoire, if you act with unbridled courage?

How does the coach develop courage? Some of us are predisposed to have a high degree of courage, which comes naturally. Others must make an intentional effort to practice courage: committing to it, determining to flex their courage muscle. So how do we strengthen that muscle? At a minimum, courage entails the ability to let go of certainty, to be able to slide in and out of the boundaries of certitude and face ambiguity and chance, as real possibilities when taking risks. When we are courageous, we intentionally develop a mind-set of expecting possible deviation and the inability to be deterministic, trusting that our judgment and intuition will help us deal with whatever surfaces in the moment. That is the emblem of the confident leader who, after having done the required due diligence, is able to live with incertitude.

Conventional thinking decrees that courage is developed one measure at a time, going from small doses to increasingly larger ones. There may be times, however, that call for an audacious move, requiring large doses of courage. When the opportunity calls, answer it. Take that giant, courageous step, make the bold move that is in line with what you want to achieve for those you lead. Do it, trusting that, in the doing, the courage manifests itself and carries you through. Courage is an emotional muscle. The more you practice it, the stronger it becomes.

Coaching is uncertain work and no matter how you show up, there will likely be those who will criticize you. We develop courage when we free ourselves from the shackles of needing the approval of others. Dare to be yourself, to stand alone, if need be: to express what you know is right, to go against conventional opinion. It's venturing out in to the rough seas of uncertainty and trusting that you will generate the courage to ride the wave of criticism. Great coaches are at peace with the prospect of failure and have developed the personal resilience to experience serious setbacks, without losing their passion and faith in the coaching process.

We enhance our ability to act courageously by thinking innovatively about ourselves—using a new framework for viewing ourselves, a framework of possibility, of being wide open to what we could be capable of undertaking, using an audacity of imagination, stretching ourselves to the full limit of what we think we are capable of and then pushing one step further until we are at our very edge. Imagine yourself there. How much courage do you need to get there?

What do you see yourself accomplishing? What is the first step you can take toward this? What do you have to do to reprogram yourself so that you own this vision of yourself? Is the vision totally transparent to you? If not, what is missing? How can you clarify it further? What are potential roadblocks? How many of these are created by you? I encourage you to use a highly inquisitive and analytical approach on yourself. For example, what are your deepest vulnerabilities, the ones you might talk about only to your most trusted friend, late at night? And what would it feel like to step out of your circle of comfort despite them and do it anyway.

Finally, the most effective process for developing courage is to cast a glance backward and forward in your life's journey. Look back over past events and memories and search for the gifts that you would never enjoy today if you had not acted with courage. Now direct your gaze to the future and determine the three major targets that you want to achieve. What are the major fears associated with these desired achievements, the fears that require the topmost courage on your part? Now think of one action—the most courageous one—that you can take today for each of these targets. This is putting your courage in motion.

Powerful coaches take bold, surefooted steps. Are you tiptoeing through your conversations? Courage is about your personal evolution—taking yourself from your shadow to your light, to the point where you are at your very best, at ease with who you are and confident that you have the fortitude to go wherever the coaching conversation needs to go. It's about shaping yourself. For the master coach, courage is a choice and a way of life.

# *CONNECTION:*
# Creating Partnerships for Inquiry, Learning, and Change

*It is an absolute human certainty that no one can know his own beauty or perceive a sense of his own worth until it has been reflected back to him in the mirror of another loving, caring human being.*

—JOHN JOSEPH POWELL, *The Secret of Staying in Love*

The coaching relationship is a unique connection that may not resemble any other in life. It is, at heart, a peer-to-peer partnership that is entered into voluntarily by both parties, based on mutual trust. This relationship becomes the medium through which the transformational process of coaching can occur. It is at once dangerous and caring, challenging and supportive.

Imagine that tomorrow you meet someone who you instinctively trust, and readily welcome into your life. This is a very special kind of person, one who looks right past the superficial parts of your personality, your typical defenses, the insecurities you've worked so hard to mask, and the failings you're ashamed to admit, let alone accept. Imagine that this person sees all of you and simply accepts you for who you really are: a unique individual who wants to be special, make a contribution, and use their most precious talents to make a real difference in the lives of others.

At the same time, this new person also sees how your personality, defenses, and insecurities get in the way of you performing at your best. This person knows when you subtly sell yourself short in your work and career, in pursuing your passions and dreams, and in your expectations for the future. And she won't let you get away with it any more. She cares about you too much to let this continue.

Because this person sees the real you and cares, she will not accept anything less from you than your very best. With a deep appreciation for who you are, this person confronts you with a level of honesty that does not allow you to deny the truth of your potential. At the same time, she recognizes clearly that this is *your* challenge—not hers. The only thing that's certain is that she is going to hold you accountable for becoming the very best version of yourself. What would it be like to have just such a person so completely on your side? Now, imagine what it would be like to be that person for others. That's what the coaching connection is all about.

It's possible, in the right environment, to simply show up and coach a stranger with positive effect. I see this in virtually every workshop I facilitate. But for the most powerful coaching to occur—the kind of engagement that can happen on an ongoing basis, within organizations—a special relationship needs to be established. Human beings are first and foremost social creatures. We exist only in relationship with others, and develop only in relationship with others.

Just as the coach needs to earn the right to serve the Talent, I also believe the burden is on the coach to create the scaffolding of this special relationship. For a leader, this involves the counterintuitive and often uncomfortable step of moving out of a hierarchical relationship and into a peer-to-peer partnership, at least for the duration of the coaching conversation. And this must be done authentically. The Talent will know if the leader is only giving lip service to this shift but covertly continuing to wield power. I sometimes call this "earning your demotion."

Most managers in today's organizations are equipped with a toolbox of solid skills for handling performance and career discussions such as giving feedback and engaging in active listening. But for managers to become coaches, they must move beyond simply having good interpersonal skills and create relationships in which the Talent is the prime focus. This enables a fundamentally different kind of conversation, one in which the coach is seen by the Talent as an equal. Coaching from a position of "I know the answers and will advise or tell you what to do" simply does not work. In order to coach, the Talent has to see the coach as a fellow human being rather than a superior, regardless of their respective positions on the organization chart and the responsibility for facilitating this shift falls largely on the more senior person.

Coaching relationships are highly personal. I don't mean that you have to be best buddies with the Talent, but you do have to authentically establish a bond of connection with each particular individual. This can seem counterintuitive, especially for leaders who come from a generation who were taught to strictly separate the personal from the professional.

Much has been written about how to coach, and there are numerous step-by-step processes available for those looking for plug-and-play solutions. But if you want coaching to be truly effective, I would advise you to put your attention first and foremost on building character and forging the coaching connection. The coaching connection is a unique and powerful relationship in which the Talent is appreciated at their best, confronted with their own talents and aspirations, and held accountable to live up to their own highest standards. If the coach can be trusted enough to form this special relationship, the Talent will be able to use the resulting conversations to learn and function at a higher level.

# Top 10 Ways to Build a Long-Term Coaching Relationship

✦✦✦

1. Have great expectations for the person being coached. Never let them sell themselves short or pursue anything but their very best path forward.

2. Accept nothing less than their very best efforts during the coaching process.

3. Help them broaden their world-view by constantly challenging their thinking and sharing alternate perspectives.

4. Coach to their values, beliefs and aspirations, encouraging them to set their own personal standards of performance.

5. Help them discover or rediscover the parts of themselves that are unique and most treasured.

6. Always treat them with dignity and respect, especially when they are not at their best.

7. Recognize and celebrate every breakthrough and victory no matter how small.

8. Always work at their most fertile growing edge.

9. Be generous with kindness and empathy when they struggle with the emotions, self-doubt and uncertainty of learning and development.

10. Give them the tough feedback that others will not.

# 10

# Appreciation

*Thousands of geniuses live and die undiscovered—*
*either by themselves or by others.*

—MARK TWAIN, *Autobiography of Mark Twain*

Sadly, appreciation is one of the most powerful yet underutilized tools in organizations today. If subjects were selected based on their ultimate payoffs, appreciation would be taught in every business school in the world. Its impact on team and organization performance is nothing short of magical. The expression of this simple sentiment has the power to dramatically increase output, accelerate change and transform lives. Yet most companies doggedly continue to practice "deficit-thinking," an approach that is heavily oriented toward the critical, focusing on discovering what's wrong with people's performance in order to fix them. How much more could be achieved through appreciation!

Appreciation is not flattery. It is much more than complimenting someone, identifying their strengths, or even giving positive feedback (though these are all appreciative in nature). Appreciation is the coaching perspective in action. It's the discipline of ignoring one's natural tendency to judge, choosing to see another at their very best (that part of them that is most precious, their essence), and describing the impact of this "best" on you and others.

Appreciation forms the foundation of the coaching relationship and creates the open space within which the coaching conversation can take place. Once the Talent feels truly appreciated (honored, respected, and valued) in the relationship, they will be willing to explore some of the aspects of their work or life that are uncomfortable or hard to look at.

## THE POWER OF APPRECIATION

The power of a positive, appreciative relationship is not a recently discovered principle of human behavior. It is a timeless, universal tenet governing human relationships. Socrates and Plato both believed that all individuals possessed inherent wisdom and talents and could make significant contributions to humanity by developing these. In modern Western thought, these ideas had a resurgence of popularity in the mid-twentieth century. One particularly notable proponent was psychologist Carl Rogers, who believed strongly that a climate of trust and respect was essential to facilitating a person's ability to develop in a positive and constructive manner and created a therapy model around this theory.

Initially, Rogers called this process "non-directive" therapy, highlighting his belief that the client, rather than the therapist, should take a leadership role in the relationship. He later changed his description of the process to "client-centered" therapy, noting that while the therapist may take the backseat in the relationship, the client nonetheless looked to the therapist for guidance. Even if the therapist tried not to direct the session, the client would still seek and find some degree of guidance. He described his sessions as supportive, not constructive, and likened the experience to learning to ride a bicycle. When you teach a child to ride a bike, you cannot just tell him how, nor can you hold him up the whole time. He has to try it out for himself and fall down a few times along the way in order to learn.

Rogers believed that the client should be responsible for determining what needed to be changed, coming up with his own suggestions for improvement, and ultimately deciding when the therapy has been successful. Thus, while acknowledging the role of the therapist in the relationship, the primary responsibility for the direction of therapy lies with the client. "If I can provide a certain type of relationship," Rogers explains, "the other person will discover within him/herself the capacity to use that relationship for growth and change, and personal development will occur."[39]

Roger's theory garnered much attention among psychologists and therapists in the 1950s and 1960s and remains influential today. But his ideas are also applicable outside of traditional counseling relationships and are invaluable to the practice of high performance coaching in the workplace. In fact, inspired by him, I like to think of my approach to coaching as "Talent-centered coaching." We human beings prefer to work with people we like, and who like us. We may say (and even believe!) that we don't need to be friends with our colleagues to get the job done but none of us wants to go to work in the morning feeling like no one cares about us. We seek out people who genuinely like us and actively avoid those we think don't like us or who are cold, unapproachable, negative, or inconsistent. Why are dogs "man's best friend"? Because they are always happy to see us. They appreciate us and love us even on our bad days. They see past our negative qualities and seem to focus on only the very best within us. And, we love them for it. Such is the gift of appreciation.

Appreciation cannot be faked. You either truly believe in the potential of another human being or you do not; either way, they know how you feel.

## A SHIFT IN THINKING

In 1987, David Cooperrider and Suresh Srivastva published a groundbreaking paper entitled "Appreciative Inquiry in Organizational Life." In it, they outlined what they called the Appreciative Inquiry (AI) method for organizational change and development. Essentially, AI takes Rogers' ideas about client-centered therapy and applies them to organizations instead of individuals. As its name suggests, AI aimed to identify, support, and perpetuate the very best in an organization through structured questioning. Cooperrider and his colleagues recognized the motivation people gain from their own success and suggested that pointing out and celebrating success in an organization, rather than focusing on its flaws and failures, results in greater improvement in overall performance. Furthermore, they argued that when suggestions for change are based on the experiences of people within the organization—things they are already doing in some way—people will be better able to relate to them and therefore be more willing to change.

According to Cooperrider and Srivastva, "organizations change in the direction in which they inquire."[40] An organization that looks for problems to fix will find and focus on problems; one that seeks its positive attributes will succeed in identifying more and more of what is already working well and focus on doing more of those things.

AI is the difference between believing that "organizing is a problem to be solved" and believing that "organizing is a miracle to be embraced."[41] It succeeds by multiplying the good behavior it focuses on, while putting aside the poor performance it no longer wants. The same principle is used in training racecar drivers: look at the wall and hit the wall; look at the road ahead and make the turn skillfully. It's not about changing people, but about inviting people to be a part of an organization that is going in the right direction.

Winston Churchill's popularity among the beleaguered British people in the darkest days of the Second World War is an excellent example of how focusing on the abilities, skills, and resources of the individuals within a group can foster a positive attitude and inspire the group as a whole to persevere. Even in the most difficult of times, we can find signs of life and hope if we look for them. The things we choose to pay attention to and the attitude we have towards change and development can make all the difference to the results we get.

# THE SIMPLEST APPRECIATION: ACKNOWLEDGMENT

Sometimes, appreciation does not need to be focused on specific attributes or strengths. One of the most powerful ways to appreciate another person is simply to acknowledge them; to see them. Genuine acknowledgment is a powerful thing. So many of us move through our days feeling as if no one really *sees* us. We rush past each other in the halls or interact on the job, but it can often seem as if our true selves are invisible to each other. Caught up in busyness, self-concern, and the hectic pace of day-to-day life, we pass like ships in the night and rarely stop to recognize each other. Hence, when someone pauses and takes even a moment to really notice us, and to communicate the value they see in us, it can have amazing positive consequences. This is just one of the reasons coaching is so effective. As previously discussed here, in our society, it is all too uncommon to experience genuinely devoted attention; when we do receive it, it can be enough to inspire us to continue to strive for great things.

Acknowledgment is more than simply greeting or initiating a conversation with someone. It is a significant verbal or nonverbal communication that the other person is seen as distinctly unique. It says, "I see you as a separate, unique individual on your own life journey but extraordinarily valuable to me and others. You are not a resource to be managed, a problem to be solved or an asset to be exploited." This perspective is the foundation and prerequisite of all great coaching conversations. The world of business has a tendency to dehumanize people, to rob them of their essential, irreducible personhood and see them instead as "human resources." Coaching owes much of its power to the fact that, through acknowledgment, it restores some degree of personhood.

Fully recognizing who someone is and what they bring to a relationship, as well as their personal experiences and challenges, can be profoundly motivating. There is a traditional

Tibetan greeting "tashi deley" meaning, "I honor the greatness in you." Acknowledgment is about honoring and respecting the people you come into contact with and giving them the gift of your attention and appreciation.

Coaching is a difficult road to travel, and the Talent deserves acknowledgment simply for walking down it. Entering into a coaching relationship is a voluntary endeavor, and any individual who consents to do so has the self-awareness to know that he or she can perform at a higher level and the courage to allow the coach to join this uncertain journey. Great coaches pay tribute to this strength of character early in the relationship.

A true coach is honest, and that also means acknowledging the Talent's struggles and the mistakes he has made in his self-management and his management of his relationships with others. But the coach is also aware that we are all, to some extent, guilty of what cognitive scientist Lee D. Ross called the Fundamental Attribution Error; that is, we generally attribute our own behavior to situational influences, but tend to blame the actions of others on character. In my opinion, true acknowledgement of another human being means correcting this fallacy. We know that the Talent has encountered difficulties and made mistakes, but we don't see their behavior as a direct reflection of the kind of person they are. We see their potential in a positive yet honest light, and encourage them to do the same by holding them accountable and insisting that they are capable of better.

Acknowledging is not synonymous with complimenting. Complimenting the Talent can be perceived as superficial or phony, especially when it only scratches at the surface of their true self. The master coach looks deeper than those attributes that are readily apparent on the surface, looks beyond personality and social graces, to see who the Talent really is, who they have been, and who they are struggling to become.

A statement of acknowledgment can take many forms, but it is always explicit about the behavior we want to point out. It can be very simple. Something as basic as using the person's first name communicates that you see them and their particular experience. A friend of mine once shared a story of a memorable boss he worked for who would greet each of his four hundred employees by name at the annual Christmas party. It made such an impact on my friend that he went back to his old boss years later to ask him how he did it. Turns out his boss didn't just happen to have a great memory. Amazingly, he cared enough to keep a binder with a picture of every employee and studied it for weeks before the party. He knew the power of acknowledgment.

## Ten Sample Acknowledgments

♦ ♦ ♦

1. You are a very interesting person
2. I enjoy working with you
3. You have a wonderfully distinctive personality
4. You are obviously a very talented person
5. I see that you are having a very good/difficult time right now
6. I think you have great potential
7. I value your willingness to confront this issue
8. I see you as quite unique
9. Your fine work has not gone unnoticed
10. I like you

If we want to coach others for exceptional performance, we begin by thinking well of them. As Leader Coaches, our goal is to assist the Talent in moving beyond a negative view of their abilities in order to heighten their awareness of their own value, strength, and performance potential. By bringing an appreciative attitude into our relationships, we assist the Talent in overcoming the limits they have imposed upon themselves, and the possibilities available to them become enormous. We are charged with the task of seeing the Talent at his absolute best, appreciating who he really is, and inquiring into his performance from that perspective. When we bring this attitude into the coaching relationship and we are unwavering in our perspective, the Talent begins to see themselves in this same light. Great coaching leaves a legacy of people who know their greatest strengths and, as a result, have the internal motivation to seek opportunities in which to deploy them.

# 11

# Great Expectations

*High achievement always takes place in the
framework of high expectation"*
—CHARLES F. KETTERING

I was twenty years old and in college when I realized that I was really quite ordinary. By then, the damage had already been done. I had spent the first two decades of my life under the delusion that I was special. Who was to blame? My mother, of course. It was all her fault. At an early age, she took me aside and told me secrets, secrets that I promised to reveal to no one. "You are very, very smart; you'll probably be the smartest boy in the school. You must be careful not to lord this over others. You will also have many friends, probably too many. You must do your best to spend time with each of them and help them in any way you can. I've also noticed that you are very fast, probably the fastest in the neighborhood. You must help others run just as fast."

By the time I was ten years old, my mother's perspective on my abilities had taken complete control of my life. I marched into school thinking I was smart, waded into relationships believing I was likable, and tried out for sports teams convinced I was athletic.

As I look back now at these three aspects of my life—academics, relationships, and athletics—I can see how blessed I was with rich experiences. They were not always perfect. I did not always make the honor roll. Sometimes I was rejected by those I considered friends. I was cut from sports teams I desperately wanted to make. But I dove into these endeavors with the confidence that I could succeed, if not this time, then next time for sure. And I succeeded more times than my limited abilities should have allowed. My mother gave me many gifts during her life but none as precious as the gift of *great expectations.*

Talent is everywhere; it just needs to be unleashed. This is the job of the master coach. And my mother had the recipe: expect the very best from people and challenge them to live up to your great expectations. As we navigate through our careers, most of our learning and development comes from those demanding endeavors that require us to stretch our thinking and abilities the furthest. High performance coaching accelerates this process by helping the Talent create the challenging developmental experiences necessary to reach this level of achievement.

Having great expectations doesn't mean the coach imposes her own idea of success on the Talent. Rather, she confronts the Talent with their own highest aspirations and strengths, and in so doing, advances them towards achieving their version of success. The leverage point of coaching is this: Figure out what another person most wants and become an advocate for them achieving it.

## THE EXPECTATION/ PERFORMANCE CONNECTION

Here's a secret that great coaches know: The expectations we hold for others are a direct predictor of their performance. And it's not because we are such excellent judges of character. In reality, it's because the opinions we have of others are self-fulfilling prophecies. No matter how they are manifested, the cues we send out are expressions of our thoughts and expectations, and they have an enormous impact on everyone around us. In the workplace, our colleagues pick up these subtle signals and respond by adjusting their behavior in accordance with our assumptions about them and their abilities. What many leaders don't realize is that by expecting less-than-greatness from those with whom they work, they are actually contributing to the less-than-great results.

Several studies that focus on teachers and students in the classroom have confirmed what I have experienced in my own work with leadership training: expectations shape performance. This phenomenon is sometimes known as the Pygmalion effect, after the Greek myth of Pygmalion, a sculptor who carved a statue so beautiful he fell in love with it and it came to life. Another name for it is the Rosenthal effect, after psychologist Robert Rosenthal who was one of the first to study the phenomenon in the classroom.

Rosenthal's Oak School Experiment was conducted in the 1960s at a small elementary school near San Francisco. He told the teachers that a particular group of children had been specially tested and had identified as intellectual bloomers who were expected to show above-average gains over the course of the school year. At the end of the year, these so-called bloomers had done just that: they showed a significant jump both in IQ scores and overall academic achievement. Their teachers also reported that these students were more friendly, outgoing, and eager to learn than their peers. The truth, however, was that the students identified as intellectual bloomers had been randomly selected from the class list. Nothing distinguished them from their peers except their teacher's expectations.[42]

The Rosenthal study is not alone in its conclusions. In his book *Self-Fulfilling Prophecy*, Professor Robert Tauber presents the results of over seven hundred doctoral dissertations and countless journal articles on stereotyping and the use of social locators, such as race, gender, ethnicity, physical appearance, age, socioeconomic status, and special needs. He found that, even in scientifically conducted studies, "what we expect, all too often, is exactly what we get."[43]

So what explains this connection between expectations and performance? "It's not magic, it's not mental telepathy," Rosenthal says. His conclusion, after continuing his research for many years, was that the likely cause came down to "thousands of different ways of treating people in small ways every day."[44] For example, teachers gave the students they expected to succeed more time, more attention, and, significantly, more approval. Even their body language—touches, smiles, nods—communicated their attitude to the students.

The same principle holds in the workplace. If you, as a leader, have a private rating system that distinguishes your "high performers" from your "low performers," or your A players from your B players—and I guarantee you do—those people know exactly how you rate them. Whether you express your assessments verbally or not, the people on your team have a pretty good idea into which category you have placed them. We're always more transparent than we would like to believe; the truth is we communicate our opinions quite clearly, often unconsciously, through a variety of verbal and nonverbal cues.

Like the unsuspecting teachers in Rosenthal's experiment, we tend to give more time and attention to those perceived as high performers and less to those we see as low performers. We will change the tone of our voice depending on whom we are addressing. We smile at our A players more often, and will make eye contact with them, while we may avoid it with those we consider B or C players. We offer more opportunities to those we expect to do well. We're more inclined to criticize low performers, but we can also fall into the trap of praising them for mediocre results, reinforcing low standards instead of demanding better. Leaders tend to provide less coaching and direction for weaker performers, and demand less work and effort from them than we would from those we consider strong performers. The list goes on.

When we think of others as unmotivated, incompetent, or unintelligent, they know it and will typically resent us for it. They will dislike working with us and will attempt to avoid us whenever possible. However, when we think of others as unique, talented, and developing, people know this as well and will respond accordingly. They will like how they feel about themselves in our presence. They will desire to work with us, and will grant us their discretionary effort. They will allow us concessions they will not allow of others. We will have gained their loyalty: a rare commodity today.

A master coach is keenly aware that his or her assessment of others matters tremendously. Of course, no leader can, or should, avoid the reality of their team members' performance. But in the role of coach, the leader strives to always appreciate the very best in people. By seeing and appreciating them, and expecting them to live up to their highest potential, the Leader Coach sets the stage for high performance.

## IT'S NOT JUST ABOUT VISION

When describing the benefits of coaching, many professional coaches' websites, publications, and other promotional material focus on "achieving a grand vision" in one form or another. I too appreciate the benefit of such an endeavor. However, for some, coaching presents a different opportunity: the opportunity to grow as a person, to become a fully functioning person in all walks of life. The great thing about coaching is that it helps us make full use of our gifts, minds, aspirations, relationships, feelings, and more, so that we can live bigger and live happier, achieve more and give more, learn more and teach more.

So, how does one become a fully functioning person through the coaching process? It involves the coach encouraging the Talent to make a deep commitment to their highest, most ambitious aspirations, engage in a process of unfettered self-examination, make decisions (and take actions) that are in the very best interests of themselves and others, and take full responsibility for these decisions (and actions) and the resulting consequences. The objective is to help the Talent step out every day with the power of knowing that they can bring all their abilities (cognitive, emotional, and physical) to bear on the complexities of work and life. And they carry the confidence of knowing that they can make alterations or corrections if the results are unsatisfactory.

# TOP 10 OUTCOMES OF GREAT COACHING

✦✦✦

*The primary objective of the coaching process is to help the Talent function at the highest level possible and, in doing so, seize opportunities that are available and constructively deal with adversities that they face. This becomes a reality when the Talent has:*

1. raised their standards of performance and career ambitions to scary heights.

2. redesigned how their precious time, attention and energy is invested.

3. eliminated those once-important practices and habits that no longer serve them well.

4. challenged and laid bare their most closely-held beliefs and assumptions.

5. set unbelievably ambitious goals for themselves.

6. de-junked their lives of incessant time-wasters, stresses, and distractions.

7. gained a greatly enlarged view of their amazing strengths and capabilities.

8. confronted and slayed the principal demons that had been blocking their way forward.

9. rediscovered their playful, creative side that had long been held in exile.

10. re-acquired a radical passion for work, life and the well-being of others.

# 12

# Accountability

*People are always blaming their circumstances for what they are. I don't believe in circumstances. The people who get on in the world are the people who get up and look for the circumstances they want, and if they can't find them, make them.*

—GEORGE BERNARD SHAW, *Mrs. Warren's Profession*

One of my professors at graduate school had a habit of asking me a particularly vexing question whenever I complained about the dreadful behavior of others in my life. No matter what I was complaining about, he always replied, "What's your part in this issue?" I still remember how that question irritated me. To a young man so sure that he was in the right and so sure that he was on top of his own game, his question was quite annoying. He just didn't get it. Why couldn't he support me in my state of self-righteous indignation? He couldn't because he was a true coach who held me responsible for my own behavior and my own life; a coach who knew that personal accountability and personal development are two sides of the same coin.

Accountability is one of the pillars of the coaching connection. As we've discussed, great coaches apply the demand for accountability to themselves, as a pillar of their own integrity, and then they apply that demand to the Talent as well. They give the Talent the gift of insisting that they are fully accountable for their own decisions and actions.

The coach cannot force accountability upon the Talent, but there is a lot she can do to encourage it. She can create an environment of intense personal accountability by modeling the accountability in her own actions and in her language, and encouraging the Talent to do the same. The language one uses is a prime indicator of the degree to which one feels personally accountable. Through shifting the way we speak, we can move away from victimhood to a place of personal power. A master coach uses the language of accountability and encourages the Talent to do the same.

Think about the language you use. Does your choice of words suggest that you hold yourself accountable for your own performance, or do you deflect responsibility elsewhere? Are you complaining about issues that you have not really done everything you possibly could to resolve? Are you blaming or playing the victim? It may seem like a small matter, but the impact of language on how you are perceived is enormous. I believe that we are always listening to those around us, almost unconsciously, and grading them on the accountability scale. We naturally attribute qualities of leadership to those individuals who assume personal accountability and discount those who do not. Take a look at the following lists. How often do you use language that is non-accountable?

## The Language of Accountability

| Not Accountable | Accountable |
|---|---|
| • I had to... | • I chose to... |
| • I cannot... | • I will not... |
| • I need to... | • I want to... |
| • I am unable to... | • I am unwilling to... |
| • I will try... | • I will do... |
| • I wish it was... | • What is possible? |
| • Who is to blame? | • I own my part. |
| • I have no control. | • What action can I take? |

The difference between these phrases may appear subtle, but if you listen closely, they speak volumes about the degree to which one takes responsibility for one's own thoughts, opinions, and actions.

As a coach, you need to be deliberately using the language of accountability, and you need to be listening carefully to the Talent's choice of expression. If you hear things like, "I had to fire him," "I cannot get along with my manager," or "I need to get more support from my team," these comments denote a lack of personal accountability and erode the Talent's effectiveness. As a coach, your job is not to listen to the Talent complain, but to help them reclaim their power.

The next time you are listening to a leader speak, listen carefully to the speaker's use of the word "I." The manner in which a leader uses this one little word reveals much about his or her inclination towards accountability. Most leaders learn early in their careers to speak in terms of "we." What should we do? How will we work together? What did we accomplish? They recognize that much of their role is to give voice to the organization's plans and performance and that, in that context, the use of "we" is most appropriate. But when it comes to their personal accountability, it's all about the "I" word. As you listen, you will quickly become adept at spotting leaders who have a strong sense of personal accountability and those who do not.

Accountability is most frequently thought of in terms of results and consequences. We typically define accountability by using words such as responsibility, answerability, and liability. I prefer to enlarge that definition by incorporating the concept of authority to act. This is a subtle, yet important distinction. It means that with the responsibility for results comes the power to take whatever actions are necessary to bring about those results. When the Talent truly believes that they are accountable and have the power to act, the coaching process becomes fully empowered.

When I hear coaches being referred to as "sounding boards," alarm bells go off. This usually means that the Talent wants the coach to act as a scratching post for their chronic complaints—about their boss, staff, customers, co-workers, and so on. Some would suggest that the Leader Coach needs to "create a safe space" for the Talent to vent and clear her issues. I disagree. The more venting (read: whining) the Talent does, the deeper they fall into the illusion of being the victim of circumstances, rather than the architect of their own future. The deeper they etch this sense of helplessness onto their self image, the more difficult it becomes for them to take personal responsibility for their own performance and the other aspects of their life which they have the power to change themselves.

Rather than being an absorbent sounding board, the master coach acts as a reflective mirror, revealing to the Talent how they can take an empowered, non-victimized stance in relationship to any situation with which they are dealing.

## CHANGING THE CONVERSATION

How does this work in an actual conversation? First, it is important to understand some theories about how individuals interact when they converse. When a person participates in a conversation, she is compelled to define herself by the role she takes on. Think about all the different roles we assume in conversations: helper, teacher, playmate, adversary, complainer, counselor—to name a few. The role we choose determines much of our behavior in the conversation. For example, when we assume the role of coach, we are defining ourselves as one who is concerned with self-development, reality, adaptation, and personal responsibility. When we choose this role, the Talent must choose a congruent role, one that can interact with the coach's area of concern, or the conversation ends. It is through this dynamic that the Talent is encouraged to assume personal accountability.

Psychotherapist Eric Berne developed a model of conversation he called *transactional analysis*. Transactional analysis provides useful ways of studying coaching conversations and the part they play in encouraging personal accountability. Berne suggested that each person chooses to interact with others from one of three patterns of thoughts and feelings he called ego states; Parent, Adult or Child:

The Parent ego state has two predominant aspects: it is controlling and nurturing. The Adult ego state, which has no relation to age, is oriented toward pragmatism, adaptation, and autonomy. The Child ego state is comprised of generally unregulated emotions and feelings. Berne further suggests that each of us has all three ego states and the ability to move between them in our conversations with others. None is considered universally superior to the others in all situations; however, the Adult is the autonomous mediator of the other states because it is in this role that the individual assumes responsibility for herself and her future.

True coaching occurs when both the Leader Coach and the Talent operate in their Adult states, with each taking responsibility for his own performance. It is all too tempting for the Talent to slip into the Child state (either rebel or victim) and the Leader Coach to slip into the corresponding Parent state (director or rescuer), but the Leader Coach must remain in his Adult state and insist that the Talent move up into his as well for coaching to be successful.

I am not suggesting that either the Parent or the Child is an inherently negative way of being. When we are in our Child, we can be playful, free spirited, and adventurous. Our Parent, on the other hand, is the piece of us that takes responsibility for a situation, steps up to make things happen, and is central to good leadership. However, there is no place for either of these states in the coaching conversation.

So what can the Leader Coach do to help the Talent move toward accountability? Simply this—when the Talent is not taking personal responsibility for his own performance and future, he will always speak from his Child. If the Leader Coach complies and speaks from his Parent, the Talent can stay in his Child for the duration of the conversation. Here is the secret: ignore the Talent's Child and speak directly to his Adult even if he initially refuses to communicate from this state. By doing this, you create dissonance and a conversation that is unsustainable. The resulting anxiety requires the Talent to either move into his Adult state or terminate the conversation.

If you have raised children, you will recognize this as a natural parenting process used to encourage children to assume more personal responsibility. Parents do this in various degrees of intensity by addressing children as young adults (assuming responsibility) as opposed to immature children (assuming irresponsibility). We ask our children to take responsibility for the role they play in any given situation; our challenge, as coaches, is to continually ask, "What is your part in the issue?" and to hold the Talent accountable for his actions.

## *The Conversation States*

# THE BOUNDARIES OF ACCOUNTABILITY

Skilled coaches have clarity regarding the boundaries of their accountability: they are acutely aware of that line that separates their responsibilities from those of the Talent. They know which issues they own and which are owned by the Talent. They know which part of the conversation they are responsible for and which part belongs to the Talent. As seductive as it may be to do otherwise, the true coach is ever vigilant not to cross that line.

When the Talent is wrestling with a very difficult issue, it is extremely tempting to dive in and help her solve her problem. The master coach knows that it is the Talent's responsibility to solve these problems. But this can be oh-so-difficult when you are oh-so-sure that you have the solution and you oh-so-badly want to be helpful. I have seen many clients struggle with a problem so intensely and vociferously that they cannot find their way out. I call this being "in the puddle." It is analogous to sitting in the middle of a puddle, splashing and shouting that you are drowning in an ocean. It is very enticing for the coach to reach down and pull the person out of the puddle. The wise coach resists this urge and challenges the Talent to stop splashing, take an honest look at his situation, stand up, and walk out of the puddle. By leaving the Talent "in the puddle" until he is ready to act, the coach demonstrates a commitment to personal accountability.

# 13

# All You Need Is Love

*Love is the only way to grasp another human being in the innermost core of his personality. No one can become fully aware of the very essence of another human being unless he loves him. By his love he is enabled to see the essential traits and features in the beloved person; and even more, he sees that which is potential in him, which is not yet actualized but yet ought to be actualized. Furthermore, by his love, the loving person enables the beloved person to actualize these potentialities. By making him aware of what he can be and of what he should become, he makes these potentialities come true.*

—VICTOR FRANKL, *Man's Search for Meaning*

"Gregg, do you like all your clients?"

I've answered a lot of questions in my career, but this was one I'd never been asked before.

"No," I said, in a rare moment of candor. Then I continued. "But, I do love them."

What I meant by this somewhat embarrassing and seemingly contradictory response is quite critical to the practice of coaching. When I said that I don't always like my clients, I don't mean that I *dislike* them, but they might not be the folks I'd choose to go and have a glass of wine with after work or spend private time with. Like many others, my critical nature leads me to make judgments, often unconscious, about people, their personalities, their values, and their motives. I truly strive to not make these judgments but, being human, I am not always successful.

Love, on the other hand, is a word without judgment, and that's critical in coaching. Liking is a judgment. How can you coach someone from this perspective? They'll know whether you like them or not. I can only approach my clients with a coach's perspective if I can love them. There is no other way for me to put aside my judgments and to see them at their best. What I'm saying is that "I care enough about you that I'm not going to worry about whether I like you or not." Accepting the other person as they are is a key discipline for the coach. When you are able to effectively coach someone that you do not particularly like, you will know you are functioning at the level of the master coach.

Love is not a term I use lightly here. I rarely use the L-word in business, but I've come to accept that there is simply no other way to describe how I feel about my clients in the coaching relationship. Perhaps one of the closest sentiments is Carl Rogers' notion of "unconditional regard." Rogers' challenge to therapists, which represented a major shift, was to accept that the regard in which they held their clients would have a huge impact on the outcome of the therapy. Similarly, I encourage coaches to recognize that if they cannot love the Talent, they will never truly be able to coach with the intensity required to facilitate profound personal learning and significant, sustained change.

For years, earlier in my career, you would never have heard me say such a thing. I tried to steer well clear of any warm-and-fuzzy emotional terminology when it came to coaching, firmly believing that such things had no place in business. I positioned the process as a practical and potent performance improvement process (which it clearly is) while minimizing the more personal aspects of this work. After all, I'd reason with myself, we are coaches, not counselors. And not just regular coaches for that matter, or "life coaches." We are *leadership* coaches whose clients are primarily senior business managers. We use words like "partnership" and "challenges," not "intimacy" and "compassion." We ask our clients to step up to a bigger game, not get in touch with their feelings.

The day I began to change my mind, I was sitting down for a wrap-up coffee with the COO of a major manufacturing enterprise, at the end of our coaching engagement. Things quickly took an uncomfortable turn. "You touched me," he said. "You really touched me." I muttered a quick "thank you" and tried to quickly change the topic to something much more dispassionate. ("Is the Super Bowl still fresh enough to provide a quick detour in the conversation?" " What about oil prices?" "How about those Yankees?") But he was not to be dissuaded. "You are not hearing me. You touched me here." This time he pointed directly at the middle of his chest. "Right here!"

At this point, I realized I had to hear him out, however awkward it felt. Clearly, something about our coaching work had not only rekindled his passion for leadership, but for life itself. He continued, "I have made three commitments, and I am living these every day. First, I have committed myself to have a positive impact on the jobs, careers, and lives of every single person in our organization, regardless of their position. Second, I have recommitted myself to be a real servant leader in my family. Third, I have committed to leave this planet a better place when my time is done." And then he said the words to which I had no response: "My heart has been opened up to a whole new world." Even today, my eyes well up with tears when I reflect on this conversation,

This COO was my client, but in that particular conversation he was remarkably coach-like with me. One of the most powerful tools of the coach is appreciation, as discussed in chapter ten, and he used that tool masterfully, despite my initial resistance to accepting it. Through his persistence, he also highlighted an important area for my own development. I realized that I had developed the strength to accept and process negative feedback but I was very uncomfortable receiving positive feedback. Many people I coach are similarly unaccustomed to receiving an honest, heartfelt reflection of their strengths and gifts.

As a coach, it's my job to remind my clients of their talents, their passions, their aspirations and their potential. That day over coffee, my client reminded me of something I really have known all along, but had chosen to forget. Coaching really is heart work—it is impossible to work that closely with someone without touching the heart along the way. So today, I unabashedly say that coaching is an act of love.

Just as coaches must love but may not like their clients; the Talent may not always like us. We may need to help the Talent understand that it is not our job befriend them but rather to help them to successfully pursue their personal agenda.

As the Beatles said, all you need is love. Coach and Talent don't need to like each other, don't have to be friends, and might never go out for a beer or share a meal together. But when they sit down to engage in a coaching conversation, love is what makes everything possible.

# CONVERSATION:
# Engaging in Dialogue that Generates Possibilities and Pathways

*We need people in our lives with whom we can be as open as possible. To have real conversations with people may seem like such a simple, obvious suggestion, but it involves courage and risk.*

—THOMAS MOORE

Picture yourself immersed in a conversation. You have lost track of time. You are keenly interested in the topic: you, your life, and your future. You and the other person are exploring all sorts of exciting ideas, testing hypotheses, and generating some cool possibilities. And you're not just talking. Several times, the talking stops and it feels perfectly natural to sit in silence. For once, you have an opportunity to reflect deeply on the things that are most important to you. You started the conversation thinking that you knew yourself pretty well but, remarkably, you have learned much about yourself in a short conversation. It has not all been pleasant. A few times during the conversation, the other person asked difficult questions you did not want to answer and shared perspectives that you knew were true but did not want to hear. But somehow, the raw truthfulness of the conversation was exhilarating. All too soon, the conversation is over. You reluctantly prepare to move on, but the now familiar voice of your companion is encouraging you to do one last thing. *Make a promise.* Not to him but to yourself. You leave with a strange sense of wonderment. That was quite an adventure. You still have many questions and concerns running through your mind, but feel the energy and thrill of being on a new pathway, a pathway of your own choosing.

What I have just described is the experience of a coaching conversation, from the perspective of the Talent. Perhaps that experience is familiar to you; perhaps it sounds new and compelling. As a coach, your job is to create a space in which other people will regularly have conversations like this. Resting on the foundation of trust in your character, you will build deep connections with people and then invite them in to a unique type of engagement—one that has the potential to change their lives in ways they cannot even imagine.

The process of successful coaching involves much more than just talking with others about their goals and dreams. While rich dialogue can uncover new ideas and generate innovative solutions, this kind of interaction alone is not coaching. Where dialogue pursues new ideas, coaching pursues entirely new attitudes and behaviors. Dialogue is the talk; coaching is the walk. How many conversations do you have during an average day? And how many of these simply function as social lubricants, helping you slide through the day without having to address the important issues facing you? How many of them really matter? A master coach understands why some conversations matter and some conversations do not. Most on-the-job conversations involve the exchange of information, instructions, advice, and opinions and have relatively predictable outcomes. While these conversations are quite suitable for normal business transactions, they are quite ineffectual in the coaching process.

Coaching conversations need to be much more potent. They are characterized by purposefulness, emotion, and direction. They are high-stakes interactions in which the Leader Coach and the Talent engage in a daringly candid conversation that can evoke a vast range of feelings. Coaching often requires the

Talent to confront sensitive issues related to their personal performance and aspirations, and challenges deeply held beliefs and ingrained practices. Over the course of one conversation, the Talent's feelings may range from exhilaration to despair, confusion to clarity, and anger to tranquility. The coach needs to be able to remain in the conversation regardless of the emotions exhibited by the Talent. Sometimes performance coaching comes perilously close to therapy or counseling; however, it is important for the Leader Coach to recognize that the future is their province, not the past. This helps keep the conversation coach-like instead of therapy-like.

My friend and colleague Bob Johnson often describes a coaching conversation as a dance, but it is a dance in which the steps are not already rehearsed. The best coaching conversations have no predictable course, and are therefore inherently uncertain and risky for both parties. They are often very simple and direct, but their outcomes are unknown. They take us outside our comfort zones and challenge us to consider new perspectives. Everything superfluous that is contained in a social conversation is burned away, leaving only the most valuable things behind. The coaching conversation does not unfold without wrinkles; it confronts the questions that need to be asked and challenges the Talent to answer them honestly.

In business, we often take a very systematic, problem-solving approach to our work. Coaching requires that we set this attitude aside and instead embark on what may be a meandering conversation. Sometimes it will feel like it is going around in circles; other times it will seem to be going nowhere. Almost all coaching conversations find themselves in the pit of despair at some point. When this happens, the wise coach knows to trust the process and resist the temptation to turn back. Keep looking for the light, and sure enough, you will emerge with your pockets full of gold.

Authentic coaching conversations can only occur when we do not assume a particular outcome. They occur when we recognize that we do not have the answers for another, but that we do hold the power to listen those answers out of him. If we let silence do some of the work, we enable the Talent to hear themselves say something that they might not know they already knew. Crucially, the conversation is a one-way street. By entering into it, the Talent has decided to explore personal changes, and the coaching relationship rests on them maintaining that commitment. If they go back on this commitment, the focus then must shift to examining what got in the way of them following through on what they committed to.

A coaching conversation can happen during a dedicated coaching session, but such conversations don't have to be confined to formal coaching sessions. Coaching can also happen "in the moment" during a spontaneous interaction in the hallway or at the coffee machine. A brief interaction in which you can share an insight, ask a big question, offer positive feedback, or engage in constructive confrontation is potentially as powerful as an hour-long scheduled conversation. What turns a chance interaction into a coaching conversation is first and foremost that it is Talent-focused. Master coaches also recognize that sometimes coaching occurs even in the absence of a specific conversation. They know that their examples can be a powerful catalyst for change, and so they strive to be coach-like in everything they do.

Most leaders don't have enough conversations with the people in their teams or their companies, and especially not conversations that are focused solely on those people. Leaders need to value conversation more, recognizing it as the lifeblood of their organizations. Conversations are to organizations as blood is to the body. If it stops flowing, the body dies. Wise Leader Coaches take every opportunity to have a coach-like conversation, whether it happens in an office, at the coffee station, in a hallway, or at the bar after work. They know that doing so keeps their organizations alive and well.

# Top 10 Coaching Mistakes

♦♦♦

1. **TRYING TO BE A GREAT COACH**
   Instead, put your energy into helping the Talent become great.

2. **WORKING TOO HARD**
   It's your job to challenge the Talent to do the hard work.

3. **NOT SAYING WHAT NEEDS TO BE SAID**
   Always walk away empty knowing that nothing important was left unsaid.

4. **NEGLECTING TO ASK THE TALENT HOW YOU CAN BE MOST HELPFUL**
   You do not own the agenda, the Talent does.

5. **ASSUMING THE TALENT IS A CHALLENGE TO OVERCOME OR A PROBLEM TO BE FIXED**
   Coaching is not a project but rather a special relationship and conversation.

6. **TALKING TOO MUCH**
   Silence and attentive listening are some of the most powerful coaching tools.

7. **OWNING THE OUTCOME**
   The Talent owns both the success and the failures; you don't.

8. **GIVING EXCESSIVE WELL-MEANING ADVICE**
   This is a very weak form of coaching that makes the coach feel good but does little for the Talent.

9. **STEERING THE CONVERSATION TOWARDS THE PATH YOU KNOW IS BEST**
   The Talent is resourceful, creative, and perfectly capable of finding their own best path forward.

10. **FINISHING WITHOUT A COMMITMENT**
    Insist that the Talent promises to advance their cause in some way.

# 14

# Coaching In the Now

*Words are secondary . . . far more important is the*
*space of conscious presence that arises as you listen.*
—ECKHART TOLLE

*ll you have is now.* I know that might sound more like something you'd hear from a meditation teacher or a new age
guru, but it's actually one of the most important pieces of advice
I give to aspiring coaches. Learn to be in the now. And it's more
of a challenge than you might imagine, especially for those in
leadership roles.

Most leaders are constantly thinking in temporal terms—and
understandably so. Every day, they are called on to make choices
with long-term consequences: setting strategies, creating teams,
hiring, firing, designing offerings and products for the customers
of tomorrow. Leaders need to master future-focused practices
such as visioning, strategic planning and large-scale change, that
help organizations thrive as they move forward. But when they
shift into the role of coach, they find themselves needing to learn
to operate in an unfamiliar place: the present moment.

Coaching is not temporal, even though it may happen over
time. In coaching, all you have is the moment you are in right
now. A coaching conversation is a series of nows. This is why
coaching programs that prescribe a series of steps don't produce
great results. When the coach is thinking ahead to the next step,
already sure of what it should be, he will not be giving his attention fully to the now. Great coaches don't assume they know the
next step, nor do they think they should. They assume that others

are capable, resourceful, and fully responsible for their own work, careers, and lives. They approach every coaching conversation with this overriding thought: "What do I need to do to temporarily subordinate my own agenda and utilize all my strengths to serve the Talent?" They bring themselves into the present and ask, in this moment, what is the most important thing I can do to be of service to the Talent? Is it a piece of feedback? An insight? A question? A constructive confrontation? A word of encouragement? Nothing at all . . . just silence? Master coaches make these choices in every moment, guided by intuition and noble intention.

## THE GIFT OF PRESENCE

Attention is a precious commodity these days, as most of us find ourselves assailed from all directions with information, distractions, and demands. Among the leaders I coach, there isn't one who doesn't feel hunted, desperately trying to keep up with the ever-multiplying requests for their time and energy. And it's not just leaders who feel this way. We're all living in a world that seems to ask more of us than we have to give. As a result, we rarely give our full attention to another person. We are almost never fully present. If you've practiced meditation or mindfulness, you may have learned how to be present in the silence of your own self for a short period of time, but have you ever tried to do the same thing with another person?

In today's workplaces we are trained and rewarded for being decisive and action-oriented. We seek to distinguish ourselves by making things happen and making them happen now. Keep moving. Don't stop. Time is money! Paradoxically, all our time-saving tools that have created our high-energy, lightning-paced world have made all too rare those little slices of time that change people's work, career, and life.

We instinctively know whether someone is present or not when we are with them. Beyond obvious manifestations of distraction like checking their phone or staring out the window, we pick up on more subtle energetic cues. They may be giving us their time, but we can feel that they are not giving us their full selves. Many of us have become so accustomed to this experience of not being fully met that it comes as a beautiful surprise when we sit down with a coach-like person who is able to give us their full attention.

Presence is an extraordinary gift that the coach can give the Talent. Before anything is said—before questions are asked, insights offered, or pathways created—the coach's simple act of being fully in that moment and available is transformational. In our workshops, we often ask participants to practice simply being present with another person for fifteen minutes. Afterwards, those taking the role of the coach describe it as difficult, humbling, and ultimately refreshing. Those being coached often say it's quite magical.

Another important aspect of presence is approaching each coaching session as if it was the first time you had sat with this particular person. That's not to say you ignore what you may already know or have experienced about the Talent, but you don't filter your experience through the past. The Talent is not the same as they were last week or last month, and this moment is unlike any other.

The master coach has embraced the discipline of presence. She knows how to set aside the distractions, both external and internal, that would take her away from being fully with the Talent in the present moment. She is deeply aware that her ability to serve rests first and foremost on the quality of her attention and intention in each of the series of nows that make up the coaching conversation.

## THE ART OF DEEP LISTENING

Being fully present is a prerequisite for deep listening. Many of us may think we're listening to someone during a conversation, when in fact a large portion of our attention is being given to the voices inside our own heads. Those voices are busy coming up with interpretations, rebuttals, comparisons, and responses. They may be whispering our prejudices or affirming our preconceived ideas. Or they may just be running through our to-do list or wondering what's for dinner. Whatever they are saying, our internal voices make a lot of noise.

As a coach, it's easy to sit in a conversation with one ear tuned to what the Talent is saying, and the other turned inward, busy thinking about what you want to say in response, what pearls of wisdom you can bring, how you feel about them, how you want them to respond, and so on. Many of these may be well-intentioned concerns, but nevertheless, they take your attention out of the moment. And the Talent will sense it. Although our inner dialogue is not visible, we all know when someone is not giving us their full attention.

We often mistakenly blame our inability to be fully attentive to others on our frenetic schedules or our overcrowded task-lists, but it is our undisciplined minds that are the problem. Our brains are literally teeming with self-talk about the complexity of holding it all together: "Craft a winning strategy . . . Call Jamie's teacher . . . Get ahead of the curve . . . Remember your assistant's birthday . . . Exceed customer expectations . . . Get that expense claim in . . . Lead organization change . . . Renew the product line . . . Call the vet. . . And fill the talent pipeline." My head hurts just thinking about it. We allow our minds to run nonstop internal stories that we make up about the people, places, and things we encounter in our daily journeys. This habit dramatically impairs our ability to create an emotional connection with others—to get present, even for a few moments.

You may not be able to turn off the voices in your head completely, but you can stop giving them so much of your attention. There are plenty of good techniques you can employ, such as "active listening," that will help you become more attentive. You may well have learned some of these in a training workshop. But repeating what the other person says, asking questions, or mirroring their body language can only take you so far if you are not truly interested in what they are sharing, and, if you still believe that the voices in your head have something more important to say. Ultimately, it is your noble intention that will make the difference. The master coach doesn't need to use gimmicks to ensure she's paying attention. She has learned to be fully in the moment and she listens intently because she genuinely knows that the answers will come from the Talent, not from anything inside her own head.

The master coach also knows that he needs every bit of his attention to really be of service to the Talent. He understands that listening is not just about hearing the words—he is focusing on a deeper level than that. He is listening beyond what is said for what is unsaid. The coach's attention is tuning in to catch the echo of the Talent's passions and aspirations, to notice small inconsistencies that may indicate deeper fault lines, to hear the resonance of their values and the dissonance that indicates a lack of alignment with those values. Unless the coach is fully present, he will miss these subtle but critical keys to hearing what the Talent is saying at the deepest level.

## MINDFULNESS AND COACHING

The idea of increasing one's mindfulness is very popular these days. This age-old meditation technique practiced by spiritual seekers has now become a popular tool for business people looking to improve their interpersonal effectiveness. Many experts also recommend mindfulness to reduce stress, anxiety, and depression while increasing satisfaction, happiness, and productivity.

So what is mindfulness? Most writers define it as having a keen awareness of one's thoughts, emotions, and sensations—not trying to alter them, but simply paying attention to them as they arise and fall away. This definition, while accurate, needs to be stretched for the coach. While being aware of his own thoughts and emotions is important, he also needs to be very aware of the Talent's thoughts and emotions.

Paradoxically, learning to be more mindful of your own thoughts and feelings is a good way to become less distracted by them during coaching conversations. As you become more familiar with the movement of your own mind and emotions, you will start to recognize their patterns. Self talk tends to follow predictable patterns, and emotions follow well-worn tracks. You'll be much less likely to get caught up in an irrelevant inner narrative or ensnared by an emotional hook if you recognize them for what they are.

Mindfulness is not the same as presence but it is a close cousin, and the two often go hand-in-hand. A good way to differentiate between these two important coaching practices is this: Presence is about *tuning out* (non-related thoughts) while mindfulness is about *tuning in*. However, mindfulness is very dependent upon presence. One cannot be very mindful unless one is first present, in the moment. Conversely, presence is also dependent on mindfulness. To be able to tune out the internal noise, you need to be well acquainted with your own mental and emotional machinery.

What does a high degree of mindfulness mean to the coach? It allows her to direct her full energy and attention to the coaching conversation. Mindfulness will also increase her ability to be empathetic, connect deeply with the Talent, and learn what is most important to them. And in being mindful, the coach models the depth of reflection and clarity of thought required by the Talent to make significant, positive changes in their work and life.

How can coaches increase their mindfulness? It's as simple as just getting into the habit of observing your thoughts and feelings. Do this without trying to manipulate them. Some thoughts or feelings may be positive. They make you feel good and you'd like to have more of them. Others may be uncomfortable, even painful, and your inclination may be to push them away. Resist both of these impulses, and just observe the thoughts and feelings from a place of detachment. Try to catch yourself when you are being judgmental. You'll know this is occurring when you start labeling things as right or wrong, good or bad, valuable or useless. As you practice mindfulness, you should expect changes, shifts, and surprises. While many of your thoughts and emotions are predictable, there will sometimes be unexpected reactions to contend with. If you practice being awake to the erratic nature of your inner life, you are less likely to be thrown off course by these moments of turbulence.

In the coaching conversation, practicing mindfulness means paying attention to the Talent as well—not just to what they are saying, but also to their unspoken cues. Be mindful of their tone, their demeanor, their body language, their energy level. Pause and reflect frequently after the Talent speaks.

## MAKING SPACE FOR SILENCE

In coaching, silence matters. Just as silence between notes allows us to hear music, the silence between the Leader Coach and the Talent allows the Talent to hear their own voice (and thoughts) with clarity. Yet silence is something many of us find awkward and uncomfortable, and we consciously or unconsciously avoid it. We immediately jump in to fill an unexpected pause in a conversation or situation, replacing the silence with superficial talk. Think about this next time you discuss the weather with a perfect stranger in an elevator.

In her remarkable book *Fierce Conversations*, Susan Scott comments on our "general discomfort with silence" in conversations, homes, and working places, and encourages her readers to "Begin to wean yourself from noise." This is no small task. Many of us are engulfed in a world of sound from the moment we wake until we close our eyes and fall asleep at the end of the day. Alarm clocks, background music, cell phones ringing, and people talking create a constant din that, when combined with the chatter of our thousands of thoughts, leaves little room to experience the power of silence.

Scott encourages her readers to "let silence do the heavy lifting." She challenges us to allow spaciousness into our conversations, space in which both parties can reflect and get closer to that which is truly authentic and of the greatest value.[45]

The master coach embraces this challenge. As coaches, our greatest effort goes not into asking or answering questions, but into providing space: a structured environment designed specifically for the Talent to identify and analyze his own thoughts. In this safe space, true reflection can take place and previously hidden solutions are discovered.

Silence is not the absence of energy; it's just the opposite. It has the power to get people to think deeper, more personally, and more broadly. It counters the freneticism of daily life and, in doing so, significantly elevates the quality of the coaching conversation. When there is silence in the coaching conversation, the Talent has the opportunity to turn their attention completely inward, switch off the need to respond/connect with others, ignore their ego and have an intimate conversation with themselves.

When the coaching conversation is a constant verbal stream, with two people sharing every thought and feeling as it occurs, there is no opportunity to pause and reflect on what has been said. This lack of reflection results in a superficial conversation. When we, as coaches, welcome silence spaces into the conversation, we allow the Talent to connect more deeply with who they really are and what their Prevailing Personal Story is. Armed with this knowledge, the Talent is better able to understand their circumstances and act from a place of personal power.

## INTUITION: THE COACH'S TRUSTED FRIEND

Tuning out the chatter of your mind and making space for silence is essential for listening to the other person. But it's also essential for allowing you to listen to a deeper part of your own self.

It gives you access to a different kind of knowledge that arises without the activity conscious reasoning—a knowledge commonly known to as intuition. Intuition is the information we have without knowing where it comes from, the gut feelings we all too often ignore or fail to trust.

Intuition has long been thought of as mysterious, even mystical. We call it a "hunch," a "gut feeling," a "sixth sense," "second sight," "clairvoyance," or even "extrasensory perception." But psychologists like Carl Jung believed it wasn't a superhuman capacity, but rather one of the four basic functions of the psyche, along with thinking, feeling, and physical sensation. Researchers today tend to agree. It is increasingly accepted that thinking operates on two levels, the conscious and the unconscious, and intuition comes from a part of the mind that is just below the surface of conscious awareness. Modern science is beginning to be able to illuminate these subterranean aspects of ourselves in ways never before possible. Today's cognitive scientists and neuroscientists are able to study things like automatic processing, heuristics, subliminal priming, implicit memory, nonverbal communication, and creativity, all of which offer clues to our intuitive capacities.

There are various models used to explain our "dual processing" capacity. Some refer to the "left brain" and the "right brain," others to the deliberate and the automatic. Psychologist Daniel Kahneman calls them two "systems in the mind," or ways of thinking, System 1 and System 2. System 1, which he characterizes as "thinking fast," is the part of our mentality that comes to quick decisions based on intuitive assumptions operating outside the realm of effortful, mindful, logical analysis. System 2, on the other hand, "thinks slow." It is the reflective, thoughtful, deliberate, rational part of our mental makeup. It moderates System 1 and decides when and where to accept the intuitive conclusions of System 1.[46]

As Kahneman argues, both systems are critical, and interdependent. Without the automated, instinctive nature of so many key functions in System 1, we would never have the energy and attention available for rational, deliberative analysis in System 2. And without System 2, we would have no means to evaluate and weigh up our System 1 intuitions. The coach needs both, but because most of us are trained to rely almost exclusively on our conscious, rational capacities, he may need to apply particular attention to learning to access and trust his intuition.

Accessing intuition requires a willingness and an ability to temporarily switch off or tune out the conscious, rational mind. This may explain why so many people claim to have their best insights while taking a shower (72 percent of us do, according to a 2014 study by psychologist Scott Kaufmann.[47] Okay, so the study was run by a company that makes bathroom fixtures, so maybe there's some bias involved here, but ask a few of your friends and colleagues and I'm sure you'll find there's truth to it as well!) The point is that intuition and flashes of insight are common when you're engaged in activities that can lift you out of the conscious mind. As Nick Stockton writes in an article on the phenomenon in *Wired* magazine, "Long drives, short walks, even something like pulling weeds, all seem to have the right mix of monotony and engagement to trigger a revelation."[48]

Intuition is a difficult term to define. I think of it as a synthesis of your experiences, your expertise, your knowledge, your feeling in the moment, that is all channeled through this amazing human mind in a way we don't fully understand. But we as coaches need to learn to trust that, because it can be a source of extraordinarily valuable information.

However we explain or account for it, intuition is one of the coach's most powerful tools. With all your conscious attention focused on the Talent, and your busy mind set aside, you leave space for impressions and insights to arise unexpectedly. Your intuition is always real, even if your interpretation of the feeling isn't always correct. And though it is never going to be the only information available, it remains a valuable tool for the Talent.

That being said, intuition should not be trusted blindly. Human beings, as we all know, tend to be biased, self-centered, and narrow-minded, and our gut feelings are too often wired to serve these less noble aspects of our nature. Sometimes, our instincts are just plain wrong. Various shadows can cloud our judgment, and sometimes we project meaning and see patterns where in fact they do not exist. An unusual degree of self-awareness is required to navigate these tendencies within oneself, and this is why the accuracy and trustworthiness of the coach's intuition is intimately connected to her character. A master coach who strives for deep integrity, healthy self-esteem, noble intention, and a high degree of emotional intelligence will find that her intuition surges as she matures in all these dimensions.

For the coach who has done the inner work to build character, intuition becomes a trusted tool. One of its most powerful functions in the coaching conversation is that it sees patterns. Einstein once wrote in a letter to a friend, "A new idea comes suddenly and in a rather intuitive way. But intuition is nothing but the outcome of earlier intellectual experience." In other words, intuition is an ability to access the wealth of past knowledge, experience, and thinking we've done, and see the common patterns in current experience.[49] As you become a more experienced coach, you will naturally accumulate a deep knowledge of how human beings operate. While you don't want to be arriving in the conversation laden down with your theories and past experiences, your intuition allows you to have access to these when they are relevant, while remaining fully present.

It has also been my observation that intuition connects the present moment to the potential of the future, and allows us to see beyond the perceived limitations of any particular situation. Jung seemed to know this, when he wrote, "only through the awareness of possibilities is intuition fully satisfied. Intuition seeks to discover possibilities in the objective situation; hence . . . it is also the instrument which, in the presence of a hopelessly blocked situation, works automatically towards the issue, which no other function could discover. . . It is constantly seeking outlets and fresh possibilities."[50] I love Jung's image of intuition always seeking bridges to new potentials and previously unseen solutions.

The fruits of intuition are what I refer to as coaching insights— the perceptions, feedback, ideas, points of view, challenges, possibilities, etc., that are formed in the moment (during the conversation) and shared, with noble intention, by the coach with the Talent. While Coaching Insights may appear to be closely related to pieces of advice, they are in fact different in several key ways. First, they are provided to stimulate new ways of thinking as opposed to solving a problem or addressing an issue. Second, they are created in-the-moment during the course of the coaching conversation and, while based somewhat on the coach's values and viewpoints, are not rooted in any particular knowledge base. Third, the Leader Coach is not significantly invested in the content and can let it go immediately.

Coaching insights should also not be our personal "war stories," tales that begin with, "It's like the time when I . . . " These rarely serve to increase the Talent's awareness of their own situation. While your coaching insight might draw on personal experiences, you don't need to draw the attention to yourself by telling a long-winded story. Instead, keep your focus on the Talent and simply give voice to what is on your mind, without censoring our true thoughts, with the express purpose of serving the Talent's development. If you cannot share what you think and feel as you listen to the Talent speak, you will be unable to guide them through the challenging and uncertain process of answering difficult questions. It's important, however, to remain detached when you share these insights, to make it clear to the Talent that you are sharing them for their benefit (not your own), and that they represent *a* perspective, not *the* answer.

Your Coaching Insights are valuable to the Talent because they are authentic reflections of your point of view; they are what you are really thinking right now. And, more often than not, they contain some key truths. Does it matter if they are sometimes incorrect? No, not at all. Given with noble intention, even an insight that is off-base offers the Talent something to react to and against and through this process helps them determine where the truth lies. The coach's job is to offer the best intuitive input he has available. Its validity will ultimately be determined by the Talent.

One final note on intuition: it is temporary. It arises in the moment, is given to the Talent, and then let go. The master coach does not cling to her intuitions or consider them general truths. She knows that they arise out of the specific instant in which they were needed and are valuable only in that context.

Communicate what you know and feel, and then allow the Talent to do what they choose with the information. Not an easy task, I know, but it is the most powerful and effective way to share information. It places the onus on the Talent to take responsibility for the choices they make.

In the chapters that follow, I'll be offering you several tools and models that you can draw on as a coach. But if they are to serve you—and more importantly, serve the Talent—they must all be made secondary to the practice of presence. Being fully present is what will allow you to sense, intuitively, which tool is the best in a particular moment or which path to take. The master coach sits fully present in the now, listening deeply to the Talent, and allowing his intuition to access both past wisdom and future potential to illuminate the pathway forward.

# 15

# The Conversation and the Story

*It's like everyone tells a story about themselves inside their own head. Always. All the time. That story makes you what you are. We build ourselves out of that story.*

—PATRICK ROTHFUSS, *The Name of the Wind*

The human brain is an amazing organ. It is comprised of the same biological matter as the rest of the body yet, remarkably, it somehow gives rise to consciousness and self-awareness. Despite years of research, scientists are still mystified by how it actually does this. Nobody really understands how living cells, sorted and connected in just the right way, can turn a weak, relatively hairless animal into a sentient being that is so extraordinarily intelligent, self-reflective, and innovative.

What we do know is that our brains have no data storage system like a computer's RAM, in which individual pieces of information are organized and warehoused and accessed at will via a catalog coding system. So how do brains organize and store information? The best (and likely only) metaphor to describe this process is story creation. We sort and store information and view the world through stories. This is one of the unique distinguishing traits that make us human. All animals have brains, but it is our ability see our world through stories that creates *the mind* and, for better or worse, has put us in charge of this planet.

The mind, like nature, abhors a vacuum. It is an incessant story-making machine that is constantly trying to make sense of the world. This is a wonderful capacity, and it serves us well, helping us create meaning and shared cultures ever since our distant ancestors gathered round their campfires to share stories. However, it has its downsides. Assumptions, beliefs, and biases are also a natural and inevitable aspect of the human condition.

## YOUR PREVAILING PERSONAL STORY

We each have a single big story with ourselves in the starring role. This story contains remnants of all the things we have experienced in life so far: who we are, what is important to us, what we are good at and not, what we mean to other people and them to us. In short, it tells us who we are, where we came from, and what is important to us today, which is why I call it our Prevailing Personal Story.

A Prevailing Personal Story may contain some faint hopes and dreams, but most are dominated by yesterday and today. We have many smaller stories about events, people, or circumstances that are less important. These are shed as time fades our memories or enhanced as our interests change. Our Prevailing Personal Story, however, doesn't change much. It is the narrative (as deep and complete as you can make it) you tell yourself about how you, others, and the world function. It is a synthesis and product of all your experiences to date and is your guidance for surviving and thriving in each system you enter. Specifically, it is your guide to:

- relating to others in your communities,
- loving and being loved,
- responding to and exerting authority,
- managing your time and energy, and
- creating defensive and offensive strategies.

Your Prevailing Personal Story is no small deal. It represents the life you have created and, as such, is central to everything you do, learn and aspire to.

There is nothing wrong with having a Prevailing Personal Story. We all have them, and we bring them to the coaching conversation. The coach needs to understand the significance of story. She needs to know that everyone she coaches has a story about themselves and it is her job to help the Talent identify and explore their stories and then create a better, bigger story. All stories are wrong, to some degree, and all stories are partial. Perceived adversaries may really be indifferent bystanders, obstacles may in fact be self-imposed limitations, and failures are often products of random unseen forces. No matter how intelligent we are, we cannot see outside of our own stories.

A skilled coach can help the Talent recognize that many of the unsatisfying events they experience in their work and life are caused by their response to particularly difficult challenges or particularly appealing opportunities and that their response is deeply rooted in patterns of behavior and implicit assumptions that emanate from their Prevailing Personal Story. Their Prevailing Personal Story gets in their way. To change their events, they need to change their story.

The master coach empowers the Talent by showing them that they have the possibility to change their story. Coaches know that our stories are not static but are potentially dynamic and can be expanded, enhanced, or enriched.

## BEYOND THE BLAME STORY

I often begin a new coaching relationship with an opening question like: "How can we best use our time together?" Most responses come in the form of stories and, fortunately, most of these stories have chapters on previous achievements, current challenges, and ambitious aspirations. Some stories are not so positive. Some are stories of blame, of powerlessness, of victimhood. These clients have created stories in which they blame someone else for their troubles—subordinates, bosses, competitors, colleagues, customers, wives, exes. We all do this to varying degrees. And when we do so, we are claiming powerlessness; we are saying that our problems or lack of opportunities are in the hands of others. Of course, I'm not denying that others do influence the environment in which we live and work. However, the great coach helps the Talent direct their energy to the things they can control and act on to positively change their environment rather than wasting it blaming others. This means helping the Talent create a new story in which the narrative is driven by accountability and possibilities.

Sometimes the Talent's stories are very faint and the coach needs to listen intently to hear them. Once heard, the coach does the Talent a great service by confronting them with the story and challenging them to craft a new, much bigger story.

Great coaches understand that, for all intents and purposes, people choose much of what we do and feel. Other people cannot make us feel happy or sad; they just give us information. That information goes into our brains where we directly or indirectly, consciously or unconsciously, choose our feeling and reaction. Much of coaching is aimed at helping the Talent realize the breadth of their decision-making power and come up with a new story that reflects this truth. Most soon recognize the considerable power they have to craft their own story of success.

# 16

# The Flow

*In rivers, the water that you touch is the last of
what has passed and the first of that which comes;
so with present time.*

—LEONARDO DA VINCI, *Notebooks*

Coaching would be much more straightforward and uncompli-
cated if one could simply memorize and follow a prescribed
series of steps in a pre-established sequence to achieve a specific
set of results. Unfortunately, it doesn't work that way. The coaching process is more improvised than scripted, more spontaneous
than structured. And, there simply aren't seven steps to become
a great coach. Instead, the coaching process follows a somewhat
circuitous path of personal assessment, reflection, probing new
territory, learning, exploring possibilities, and implementing profound personal changes.

That being said, it is possible to identify three broad phases
through which many coaching conversations travel. I call these
Discovery, Creation, and Commitment. In the Discovery phase,
we explore aspirations, values, and the current situation, taking
participants to new depths; in Creation, we generate new possibilities, opportunities, and perspectives; and in Commitment, we
forge new action plans and accountabilities.

The Leader Coach must navigate these phases as the Talent
takes on the often rough and unpredictable waters of personal
and professional change. Because these phases are distinct, they
are often misinterpreted as a static, linear model for undertaking

coaching conversations. Understanding these phases can help the coach to orient herself, but she must always remember that coaching conversations rarely follow these phases sequentially and often circle back through earlier phases to explore new information or possibilities. The coaching flow is, as a client of mine once described it, "an unguided pilgrimage to my best and scariest future."

# DISCOVERY

This phase is aimed at helping the Talent learn about themselves and their interactions with others. The coach is not teacher or mentor but rather a fellow learner. In this collaborative learning partnership, the Talent may explore their:

- **Core personal values,** to remind themselves of what is most important to them in work and life.

- **Aspirations,** to gain clarity on the most desirous, ambitious futures.

- **Prevailing Personal Story,** to determine level of life satisfaction and potential for dramatic changes/shifts.

- **Relationships,** to determine which add to the life and which detract.

While many people profess to love to learn, learning about oneself is often a very challenging and sometimes painful process, especially if our Prevailing Personal Story is threatened. It is part of the coach's job to hold a space for this process, with compassion, and gently but firmly keep the Talent on course.

# CREATION

Creation is much more than simply brainstorming ideas and selecting the best option. It is about challenging assumptions, stretching ambitions, examining unthinkable possibilities, considering radical options and previously abandoned ideas. In this phase the Talent is challenged to become the sole author of their life story and to create the job/work/life/relationships/ priorities/career of their choosing that best serves their desire. That need or desire will vary between individuals, but it might include the desire to express themselves creatively, the desire to serve others, the desire to build something significant, the desire to create their masterpiece, or the desire to live in peace and comfort.

## COMMITMENT

Unless something changes, coaching is just talk. The Commitment phase is dedicated to helping the Talent close the gap between their good intentions and personal change by making specific commitments to action. It is the part of the coaching conversation in which the Talent chooses a new perspective and a new way of operating, and commits to enacting the necessary change in his life.

This is a much more profound process than simply deciding to do something new. It doesn't mean saying, "Tomorrow I will make my relationship with our VP of Operations better." Rather, it is about engaging in a personal process of transition in the moment. This requires the Talent to recognize the ways in which they own the situation, and realize that they need to change themselves, not the other person. Commitment requires that the Talent take a first step toward change right then and there, and that they hold themselves accountable for that decision. Commitment is fluid, not static; it moves with the Talent as they need to change.

Exploring some form of the four-part question; "What are you prepared to learn, invest, risk and sacrifice?" often helps the Talent gauge their true level of commitment to a decision.

While the Leader Coach is interested in long-term goals (and other grand plans), he can often be most helpful by challenging/

encouraging the Talent to identify and take the most potent first step. Often, this is the one, defining action that will launch them on to a new pathway going forward, possibly beyond the point of no return.

The greatest challenge of this final and most difficult phase of coaching is for the Talent to recognize that it won't be easy. There are many forces in the world trying to push them back into their previous performance patterns. There will inevitably be times when the Talent will be blown completely off course. True commitment is the ability to get back up and keep going, regardless of setbacks. Commitment cannot be rushed into, but once it has been reached, it demonstrates the true power coaching has to deliver sustainable performance improvement.

# CRITICAL PATH COACHING

♦♦♦

**C**ritical Path Coaching is a disciplined process aimed at helping the Talent close the gap between their good intentions and their actions. It challenges the Talent to identify and commit to those actions that will most likely ensure they achieve their goal, even if they may be difficult. While this process may appear to be a step-by-step, linear planning process, it is designed to help the Talent confirm and deepen their commitment to the outcomes of the coaching. The underlying question is this: *"Are you really prepared to do the things you know you need to do to achieve what is most important to you?"* The *Critical Path Coaching Process* involves working with the Talent to help them define their most promising steps forward as follows:

**One Defining Action**—"What act will set you on a completely new course, maybe past the point of no return?"

**Two Shifts in Beliefs**—"What shifts in assumptions or beliefs do you need to make going forward?"

**Three People Actions**—"Which people are most critical to your success and what do you need to do with them?"

**Four New Habits**—"What new practices do you need to immediately incorporate into your day-to-day routine?"

**Five Resources to Access**—"What financial, physical, informational, and collaborative support will accelerate the process?"

# 17

# The Three Coaching Power Tools

*Your words, your thoughts, your imagination:*
*powerful tools. Remember that and use them wisely.*

—DONALD L. HICKS, *Look into the Stillness*

The following Three Coaching Power Tools are presented to help you increase the quality of your coaching conversations. They are not intended to be always used exactly as presented but to prompt and guide your thinking as you as choosing the best way to serve the Talent.

## POWER TOOL #1: BIG QUESTIONS

Coaching is based on the assumption that people can ultimately determine their own best path forward. Great coaches understand that asking a provoking question is far more valuable to the Talent than any amount of advice could ever be. A well-posed question is a powerful thing. Coaches ask questions not simply so they can gain information but, instead, to help the Talent discover new aspects of themselves, create fresh possibilities, and commit to potent action.

I have found that questions that are short, simple, open-ended, and challenging are the perfect tool to force the Talent to look for their own answers, answers they already have within themselves. By asking a question, the coach avoids offering direct guidance or trying to solve the Talent's problems for them. Remember, coaching is non-directive. The more the coach attempts to help, guide, relieve pain, avoid anxiety, remove stress, or solve problems, the less effective she will be. Instead, a master coach asks questions that challenge the Talent to dig deep within and find their own personal truths. Often this exercise results in the Talent realizing something they didn't know they already knew and making a significant change based on the newly discovered knowledge.

The role of the Leader Coach is simply to ask the questions that bring those answers out. There are an infinite number of questions the coach can ask, and the task is to find the ones that inspire the most productive self-reflection in the Talent at a given moment. The master coach poses questions that go deep, open up unexpected perspectives, and provoke change. Intuitively, he or she will know what these questions are; they are usually the most obvious ones and the ones that first come to mind.

Children do this extraordinarily well: Where do babies come from? Why can't I play with that man? Why doesn't Mommy sleep here anymore? Where does God live? Have you noticed how we often become uneasy when confronted with the questions of a child? All of a sudden we are not talking about dinosaurs, SpongeBob SquarePants, bedtime rules, table manners, or the dangers of the basement stairs. The child has sparked a different kind of conversation requiring a different kind of thinking and we can't slide by with pat parental responses. They force us to examine our own assumptions, beliefs, and values and to express what we find in words that a child can understand—no easy task!

In coaching, the power is in the question. Phrased in the right way, questions can jolt the Talent into recognizing an unacknowledged truth or a new perspective on their situation and expand their understanding of their own potential. Answering tough questions challenges the Talent to identify and live out their most important values, to pursue their aspirations, and seek to become the very best version of themselves.

I like to think of these kinds of questions as "Big Coaching Questions." A Big Coaching Question has several important distinguishing characteristics. It:

- is simple, clear and open-ended,

- usually takes considerable thought and time to formulate a response,

- rarely starts with "Why" as the responses to these questions are more useful in counseling and similar helping processes,

- does not convey advice (e.g. "Have you tried X?"),

- ignites fresh thinking,

- and, most important, provides an answer that is more important to the Talent than the Leader Coach.

In my years working as a coach and training others, I've come up with a list of 60 Big Coaching Questions that coaches can draw on. These are not a formula to be followed, but rather, a source of inspiration and a toolkit that can be accessed, intuitively, when the right moment arises.

# THE 60 BIG COACHING QUESTIONS

✦✦✦

## Discovery/Learning

1. How can we make this conversation most useful to you?

2. When you are at your very best, what are you doing?

3. What excites you most about your future?

4. For what are you most grateful?

5. For what do you want to be known?

6. What can you do better than most everyone else?

7. Are you currently doing your best work?

8. Where have you achieved your greatest success?

9. On what do you waste your time and energy?

10. What are your most ambitious aspirations?

11. If you do not change, what is likely to happen?

12. What distractions are impeding your best work?

13. Who do you most frequently blame for your problems at work?

14. What is the most important unanswered question facing you right now?

15. What relationships are most important to you?

16. What talents do you know you have but are not using?

17. Whom do you serve?

18. \What kind of person or leader do you want to be?

19. What did you do yesterday that is worth talking about today?

20. Is your best work ahead of you or behind you?

# Exploration/Creation

21. What is the most exciting outcome you can imagine?
22. How can you do more of the work you love?
23. What will happen if you take your foot off the brake?
24. What is an entirely different way of looking at your situation?
25. How would others describe your performance and your potential?
26. To shift to a new level of performance, what skills and competencies do you need to master?
27. What would need to happen for you to feel powerful and in control?
28. What thoughts, attitudes and habits no longer serve you well?
29. What would you do if you had unlimited resources?
30. How can you use more of your natural talents every day?
31. What future do those who care about you most want for you?
32. What is the riskiest, scariest option?
33. What do you do very well, love to do, but no longer need to do?
34. If failure had minor consequences, what would you do?
35. In what ways can you shine a brighter light into the work and lives of others?
36. What would it take to shift your performance to a whole new level?
37. What is the most important thing you have learned about yourself recently?
38. How can you become more mindful of the people around you?
39. How can you have a more positive impact on those you care about most?
40. What will make you happy?

## Action/Execution

41. What specific outcomes are you expecting?

42. How important are these outcomes to you and others?

43. What is the most potent first step you can take?

44. What milestones will you use to measure you progress?

45. What difficult conversation needs to happen?

46. Whose support is most valuable?

47. To whom will you be accountable?

48. What promises will you make to yourself and others?

49. What actions do you need to take but are avoiding?

50. What will you do when you encounter unexpected obstacles?

51. What one personal change will result in the biggest benefit?

52. What do you need to learn to accomplish your goal?

53. What are you prepared to invest, risk and sacrifice?

54. What short-term breakthroughs will energize your undertaking?

55. What new practices will you put in place to make sure the changes are enduring?

56. How can you get others eager to partner with you?

57. How will you know when you are on the new road?

58. What are your best sources of feedback to measure your progress?

59. What do you need to do so that you will have no regrets?

60. How will you celebrate your success?

# POWER TOOL #2: COACHING PATHWAYS

While questions are the first approach of the coach, they are not the only tool at her disposal. Sometimes the coach is also called on to share ideas, observations, and thoughts. After all, we each bring our own unique perspective, rich with knowledge, talent, skill, and experience to every relationship we enter. We would not fully serve the Talent if we withheld any of these precious resources from our conversation. By doing so, the coach provides the Talent with something to react to and thereby dive deeper into their own best thinking. As coach, you have an incredible wealth of experience and knowledge that can benefit the Talent and it is valuable to share this. Seasoned coaches draw upon their extensive experience and deep intuition to provide the Talent with discussion pathways that may be very fruitful for them.

While listening deeply to the Talent, the coach will often recognize a familiar human pattern and have an intuitive insight into a potentially fertile pathway for the coaching conversation to follow. This does not mean she knows where that pathway will take the Talent, but she recognizes enough of the terrain through which the conversation is taking them to guide it in a certain direction. Intuition, as discussed in chapter fourteen, can be interpreted as an unconscious ability to perceive patterns. And individual journeys, while each unique in their nuances and details, follow broad patterns that an experienced coach learns to recognize. Over decades of working with people, I've identified the these twelve common patterns that coaching conversations may unearth. I call them "pathways" because they are not prescriptive in their steps, but rather, represent general directions to explore. They allow the experienced coach to act with *informed* intuition. *The 12 Coaching Pathways* are presented to help coaches broaden their repertoire of potential insights that may be valuable to the Talent. Each pathway comes with a "potential indicator." These are the clues the coach may notice as the Talent speaks that alert her to the most relevant path to pursue.

# THE 12 COACHING PATHWAYS

## 1. ENVISIONING A BIGGER GOAL, LIFE OR LEGACY
✔ *Potential indicator:* The Talent is dissatisfied with status quo and feeling stuck.

## 2. ALIGNING BEHAVIOR AND ENERGY WITH VALUES
✔ *Potential indicator:* The Talent seems consumed with busyness and hard work, but has little passion and job satisfaction.

## 3. STOPPING SELLING ONESELF SHORT
✔ *Potential indicator:* The Talent seems inordinately self-deprecating and unwilling to pursue ambitious objectives.

## 4. HOLDING ONESELF ACCOUNTABLE
✔ *Potential indicator:* The Talent seems to frequently blame others for their problems and lack of success.

## 5. TAKING ACTIONS THAT ARE BEING AVOIDED
✔ *Potential indicator:* The Talent is highly motivated to achieve something but seems unwilling to move forward.

## 6. USING TALENTS THAT HAVE NOT YET BEEN TAPPED
✔ *Potential indicator:* The Talent has demonstrated considerable success in other dimensions of their life.

## 7. FACING UP TO REALITY
✔ *Potential indicator:* The Talent does not seem to really believe their own story.

## 8. GAINING FRESH PERSPECTIVES
✔ *Potential indicator:* The Talent expresses powerlessness or apathy, or sees only one path forward.

## 9. CHOOSING OPTIMISM, CONFIDENCE, AND HAPPINESS
✔ *Potential indicator:* The Talent lacks energy and appears forlorn.

**10. MOVING PAST MISTAKES AND FAILURES**

    ✔ *Potential indicator:* The Talent is reluctant to make ambitious plans for the future.

**11. INTEGRATING COMPETING ASPECTS OF WORK AND LIFE**

    ✔ *Potential indicator:* The Talent is very busy and very unhappy.

**12. CLARIFYING BOUNDARIES**

    ✔ *Potential indicator:* The Talent appears to be overly concerned about what others think of them.

# POWER TOOL #3: THE 10 KEY CONVERSATION INTERVENTIONS

There are moments during the course of the coaching conversation when a question does not need to be asked nor is a pathway followed but something needs to be injected into the conversation so it can move forward. An assumption needs to be tested, a failure needs to be seen as a lesson, a behavior needs to be named, an affirmation needs to be heard. Great coaches use every tool at their disposal in service of the Talent. The following list is presented to help you broaden your repertoire of potential conversation interventions.

## 1. INCISIVE INQUIRY

    ✔ Intense testing and challenging of assumptions, beliefs, and values.

## 2. RADICAL REFRAMING

    ✔ Extracting new meaning from circumstances by exploring alternate points of view.

## 3. PERSONAL PERSPECTIVES

    ✔ Providing in-the-moment reactions and feedback.

### 4. PROVOCATIVE PARAPHRASING
✔ Interpreting and articulating what is really being said.

### 5. DEFYING IMPOSSIBILITIES
✔ Thinking the unthinkable and imagining the unimaginable.

### 6. SCENARIO EXPLORATION
✔ Preparing for uncertain futures through simulation and systems thinking.

### 7. REFLECTIVE SILENCE
✔ Spending time in quiet deliberation and contemplation.

### 8. APPRECIATIVE INQUIRY
✔ Energizing affirmations that focus on strengths, successes and positive change.

### 9. CHALLENGING CONSTRAINTS
✔ Asserting that all achievements are reached in the face of limitations, restrictions, and deficiencies.

### 10. INSPIRED VISUALIZATION
✔ Conceiving surprising and unexpected possibilities using metaphors, imagery, and story creation.

As I have said many times in these pages, I firmly believe that great coaching results more from who you are than what you do. However, it is also important to be able to communicate that information to the Talent effectively. The Big Questions, Coaching Pathways, and the 10 Key Conversation Interventions are all powerful tools that allow you to bring important, provocative subjects to light in the coaching conversation and effect development and change in the life of the Talent. Being fully present in the coaching conversation, your intuition will guide you as to which of these tools is the best fit, in any given moment, to unlock the greatest possibilities for the Talent.

# 18

# Constructive Confrontation

*Everyone wants one person in the world to whom they can tell the truth and from whom they will hear the truth. Become that person.*

—SUSAN SCOTT, *Fierce Conversations*

At twenty-five years old, I was an engineering technologist in an aluminum smelting plant and I had just been made a team leader. Perfect! The world was unfolding exactly as it should. I had worked my tail off on some key projects to earn this promotion. I deserved it. I clearly had enormous potential and extraordinary political savvy.

Martin was a senior engineer who had been in the department for over thirty years. A somewhat stately gentleman and a good engineer, but he was going nowhere. He was what we referred to back then as "potential realized." Martin and I were not especially close, as it was obvious that he had little political power and that my time could be better spent cultivating more profitable relationships elsewhere. But I will never forget the moment Martin stepped in front of me as we were leaving a staff meeting and, blocking my exit, asked if I would mind staying behind for a bit.

As the room cleared, he invited me to sit down and he sat with me. He spoke clearly and directly: "I like you, young man, and think you will have a fine career in this company, but I really wish you could see yourself in these meetings. Whenever you speak to senior managers, you come across as a real apple-polisher." (Actually, he used a more direct and colorful term.)

Then he added the words that rocked me to the core: "People laugh at you behind your back." It felt like a sledgehammer had just hit my stomach. I couldn't speak. I remember mumbling an unintelligible "Thank you." This was incomprehensible. Coming from anyone else, I would have immediately engaged in a spirited debate about the realities and necessities of organizational politics, however somehow I knew Martin wasn't there to argue the topic or to criticize me. I knew instantly that, for some reason, he cared enough about me to tell me something that others would not. He cared enough to confront me with reality.

I would like to tell you that Martin became my career-long mentor and we became life-long friends because of that conversation, but neither of these things happened. In fact, we never spoke of that topic again. But that moment, that painful moment, touched me in ways I am still discovering. I spent three years in that organization, and I remember working on some very interesting projects and having some great experiences; however, it was that brief moment in time that put an indelible mark on my work and my career. With the best of intentions, Martin shared with me the one thing he thought I really needed to know. He gave voice to a huge blind spot, even though it was probably very difficult for him to do so and with no motive other than helping me on my career journey.

In this brief encounter, Martin exemplified one of the hallmarks of the master coach: the willingness to engage in constructive confrontation. The word "confrontation" is usually defined as a conflict between people's beliefs and opinions. I prefer to define it as a courageous encounter with the truth—whatever that truth might be.

Feedback is one of the most powerful influences on performance, learning, and career development, and providing effective feedback is an essential competency for leaders at all organization levels. However, because providing feedback often involves differing perspectives, emotional spikes, and important career decisions, it is also one of the more difficult tasks for leaders. At its best, feedback is a potent tool stimulating honest self-reflection, insight, and personal improvement. At its worst, it creates an environment of discontent, conflict and unhappiness.

The Leader Coach is not a dispassionate judge who enumerates the Talent's countless flaws, nor is she a sightless cheerleader blindly dispensing plaudits. While much of the emphasis in this book has been on appreciation, on seeking to identify the best in others, coaching is not warm and fuzzy coddling. In fact, effective coaching requires us to challenge others with excruciating honesty and candor.

Telling the truth is a perilous endeavor for both the receiver and the teller. Coach and Talent will be continually tempted to form a silent partnership committed to avoiding pathways that are uncomfortable, uncertain, embarrassing, or unknown. We tend to break this silence only when the degree to which we care for another exceeds the risk and discomfort in doing so. We risk confrontation when we care deeply about another person and when we genuinely want to see them thrive. This is the paradoxical gift of confrontation. We confront others when we love them enough to not *not* speak the absolute truth. Some people call this "telling the truth in love." Great coaches care enough about the Talent to suffer the pain of this quality of truth-telling.

How often do you tell others the truth, the real truth—what you are really thinking, feeling, and wanting and what you see in them? Give this a moment of serious consideration. Reflect on your key relationships and as you think of each, consider how honest you have been in that relationship recently. How truthfully have you communicated your thoughts, both negative or positive, to your family members, friends, or coworkers?

## COURAGEOUS ENCOUNTERS

Often, the primary role of the coach is to test and disrupt the Talent's Prevailing Personal Story. The master coach is skilled in the art of confrontation. He recognizes that he is likely the only person who will confront the Talent's ideas, perspectives, and assumptions, and in so doing, enable them to find possible new ways of acting and thinking. To the great coach, confrontation means holding up a mirror so that the Talent can come face-to-face with their perspective on their current situation, abilities, aspirations, and potential, and move beyond the limits they have set for themselves.

The word "confrontation" usually evokes the notion of providing negative feedback or the feeling that we are going to be challenged by or faced with an enumeration of all the things we fear we are doing wrong. But what if confrontation was a positive action? Consider what it would be like to confront someone with his own natural talents and potential. Confrontation is equally about challenging the Talent with the good stuff. In fact, rather than focusing on their weaknesses, great coaches spend more time confronting the Talent with his own potential and then challenging him to live up to that potential.

Ironically, for many of us it is as difficult, if not more so, to be confronted by our own greatness as it is to face our faults. You cannot un-ring a bell. Once confronted by our gifts and talents, we can no longer deny the magnitude of our potential. Suddenly, there exists an unspoken obligation to rise to the occasion. A tension has been created between what is and what is possible. However, many of us silently collude with others to not be confronted. We establish a relationship based on pseudo-mutuality; the unspoken contract that says "I won't expect more from you if you don't expect more from me."

Most of us believe that we're truthful. During leadership development workshops, I often ask participants to rate themselves on their personal level of honesty within their organization. I ask them to declare how frequently they tell the complete truth. By far, the most popular response is "almost always." It's interesting, however, that when I poll others in their organization about how frequently they are told the complete truth by their leaders, I most often hear a response of "sometimes." Why the gap?

We may avoid telling the complete truth more often than we're aware. It's not that we are intentionally dishonest (though recent history has certainly been rife with enormous integrity breakdowns in senior corporate management), but rather, that we are trained and conditioned to communicate what we believe to be appropriate in the circumstances. Over time, this business-speak pervades our communication processes and significantly impairs our ability to be seen as consistently honest. In fact, evidence suggests that tempering the truth is a behavior learned from an early age and can become largely automatic. As children, we were told to think before we spoke, and when we didn't, we quickly learned the consequences. If we weren't careful with our words, we could anger our parents, embarrass ourselves, lose friends, and incur the wrath of teachers. Therefore, as adults we are accustomed to analyzing our thoughts before we share them and holding back the pieces which we decide are not appropriate. We carefully manage our communication with others, sparing both parties the anxiety and discomfort that so often accompany unwelcome or uncomfortable truths.

Striving to be considerate of another's feelings is one way we show our respect and demonstrate that our intentions are noble. Consider for a moment that our desire to not hurt others may actually be the most hurtful thing we can do. When our words are anything less than completely truthful, our coaching effectiveness is impaired. It is only when our best intentions are paired with unusually truthful communication that high level coaching occurs.

## THE POWER OF TRUTH

Truth is a powerful tool. It is the fuel of high performance coaching. It can free someone from disillusionment and allow them to set a new course. It can expose an unrecognized lie, or it can jolt someone out of mediocrity and into a whole new way of living that they might never have imagined or dreamed of. It often is the catalyst that propels the average performer to much higher levels. Truth can open new reservoirs of untapped potential. When the coach curbs the truth—positive or negative—coaching stalls.

When I catch myself withholding the truth from a conversation, my instinct is to justify this behavior by telling myself that I am really doing it for the other person's own good. Upon reflection, however, I find that my real motivation is an uncomfortable blend of both arrogance and fear. My arrogance is in play when I believe that the Talent is so fragile that they can't handle hearing something I believe to be true. But am I really so powerful? Are they really that breakable? What's also going on is that I'm usually simply afraid. My fear comes to the forefront when I convince myself that sharing the truth will produce some kind of emotional outburst from the Talent, making them unnecessarily uncomfortable. In reality, I am protecting myself from the discomfort of intense emotional involvement.

Think about an instance in which you withheld the truth. What was the story you told yourself about why that was the right thing to do? Then ask yourself, was it really true? Or were you, on some level, being self-protective?

What opportunities for growth is the Talent missing if you as a coach lack the courage to speak? What if you were the only person to ever dare offer honest words to someone who truly needs to hear them? Coaching is too important to dance around doling out vague hints about what is really on our minds.

Imagine you were the Talent and your coach wanted to tell you her honest (and probably accurate) perspective on a situation that concerns you? If you later learned that she held back, what would you think of her? Would you think she was being helpful or unhelpful? What would you prefer she do?

The master coach associates truth with love and confrontation with kindness. Truth is inextricably tied to noble intentions.

When we realize that truth is related to caring about someone holistically, we can appreciate the privilege and importance of being the bearer of such truth to the Talent. Telling an affirming truth is as important as telling an admonishing truth, and a great coach is committed to both.

Coaching is about removing the obstacles that lie in the way of each person achieving the greatness within him. Confrontation and courageous encounters with truth are parts of this process. Recently, a woman shared with me how her boss had remarked that a certain guest speaker would never be invited back again. Apparently the speaker had talked too long and ignored the time allocated to him. She said to her boss, "But he will never know the reason why he isn't invited here again. Maybe he will continue to make this mistake everywhere he goes. What if you were the only person who ever decided to tell him the truth?" How often do we miss an opportunity to remove a hindrance to higher performance because of reluctance to confront?

When we interact with someone regularly, either socially or at work, we develop a certain instinct about them. You might call this a hunch, or an intuition, as discussed in chapter ten. As often as not, these hunches are correct, but how frequently do we act on or express them? My instincts might tell me that my friend is drinking too heavily. Will I say anything to him? Will I express concern or even blurt out what I'm thinking? What would happen if I did? Am I simply a fear-monger or am I expressing real and instinctive concern for his wellbeing? Risky business, isn't it? It's much easier to recognize the truth than it is to take the uncomfortable step of voicing it, and risk looking foolish or finding our comments unwelcome.

In his popular book *Blink*, Malcolm Gladwell sheds light on this ability to know something without making a conscious effort to do so. His research suggests that when assessing a situation, the brain works on two levels: conscious and unconscious. At the unconscious level, we can reach a conclusion in seconds, without even knowing we have done so. The brain sends signals through sweat glands, for example, long before we consciously come to the conclusion that something is amiss. Gladwell uses the example of a handful of art historians who experienced this phenomenon when confronted with a marble statue purported to date from the sixth century B.C. They instinctively knew it was a fake, even though scholars and scientists had laboriously worked at a conscious level to wrongly conclude it was genuine. Gladwell's book supports the notion that we can act on that impulse, that certain intuition, with a high degree of accuracy.[51] More often than not, however, we prefer to push these rapid conclusions aside rather than take a chance and ask a dumb question. We procrastinate and take our unspoken thoughts home.

Why do we not ask more "dumb" questions? We seem to assume that if we do, others will think less of us (or more likely, that we will think less of ourselves). If we are the only ones asking questions like this, everyone else must be much smarter than us. We don't want to lose face, be ashamed, or seen as ignorant by our peers, so we wear a mask of perfect comprehension, pretending to understand. And yet, as a coach I have learned that we need to welcome, not fear, a response to a well-meant comment or question, even if it is negative. Our words tell the Talent that we care enough to risk looking foolish and having to deal with an uncomfortable response. If we didn't care, we wouldn't invite the possibility of embarrassment.

Part of the difficulty in telling the truth is that most of us are not fully aware of what it is we are feeling in the moment, and even if we were we would be hard pressed to articulate it. This is why after a particularly taxing conversation, we spend time replaying it over in our mind, trying to decipher exactly what happened and then often wishing we had said or done something differently. Even when we do notice how we feel in the moment, we are often afraid to voice it for fear of hurting another, or we avoid it because we don't want to feel uncomfortable. Rather than take a risk we choose to say nothing, or communicate a watered- down version of what we are really thinking. Often we blatantly disregard our truest thoughts, much to the detriment of everyone involved in the conversation.

If only recognizing the truth were easy! Then we would all speak it more. However, telling the truth requires that we advance our conversation from the level of politeness (where the unspoken contract is "don't push me and I won't push you") to a higher level of honesty ("I care about you enough to risk saying this because I feel you will ultimately benefit from hearing it").

Confrontation is difficult because it requires three fundamental considerations. To confront someone, we must first be able to recognize our own thoughts and feelings in a situation. We then need to trust that our feelings contain valid information worthy of sharing. And finally, we must assess whether sharing our real thoughts and perspectives is worth the risk.

Once we know what we have to say and that we have to say it, the next question that often arises is, how we can say it best. But this is not what we need to focus on. The conversation we need to have is often the instinctual conversation. We don't need to search for the "best" or "most appropriate" response and we don't need to worry about getting it right—it's our perspective, uncensored and uncut, which is needed. As much anxiety as there can be behind its telling and receiving, when confronted with the truth, people generally feel honored and special. Though we often deny the truth when just in our thoughts, it's remarkably easy to recognize once it has been given voice. This doesn't mean we always want to hear it, of course, but for the most part, we have respect for the fact that someone had the courage to voice it.

When I look at the people who have most positively impacted my life, I find that many of them had that unique blend of courage and love that enabled them to tell me things that others would not—things I needed to hear. They confronted me because they cared about me. It is my experience that most of us have had at least one person in our lives who has done this for us and has been remembered and cherished for it. The master coach sees it as his or her calling in life to be the person who cares enough to confront others with such truth.

## JUST ONE CONVERSATION

When we have a coaching conversation with someone, we can't be giving all our attention to a different background conversation in our heads. What we are saying and what we are thinking need to be essentially in alignment. This does not mean that we simply blurt out our thoughts, which can come across as choppy and reactive. Engaging in coach-like confrontation means mastering the art of translating our inner thoughts and perspectives into communication the Talent can hear.

Even if we doubt the value or relevance of our internal conversation, we still need to find a way to share it effectively with the Talent. If we do not, a part of us will be disengaged and unable to focus fully on the spoken conversation. Sharing our internal conversation is a way of keeping ourselves engaged in the interaction. Even if what you put out there does not ring true for the Talent, speaking up has two important effects: it keeps you fully present in the conversation, and it gives the Talent something to react to.

It is not the role of the coach to determine the value of the information we give. The coach's job is to put it out there, with noble intention, for the Talent to use or not use as she sees fit.

Pay attention to your next several conversations, whether with friends, family, or those in your professional life. Is the conversation you are having out loud the same as the one going on in your head? Notice if and when the conversation separates. What truths do you know that you are withholding from the external conversation? When we conduct two conversations simultaneously, something is going on that needs our attention.

# The Inner Conversations of the Coach

◆◆◆

## The Conversation Before the Conversation

○ What are my intentions? Are they truly honorable? Do I need to do some work here?

○ What assumptions am I making? Are these reasonable? What do I need to confirm or disconfirm early in the conversation?

○ Am I looking forward to the conversation? If not, why not? Do I need to do some work here?

## The Conversation During the Conversation

○ What is the Talent's Prevailing Personal Story? Is a bigger story possible?

○ What is the Talent avoiding? What am I avoiding?

○ Am I fully present and engaged? Do I need to do some work here?

○ Whose approval am I seeking?

○ Which Coaching Pathway might be most helpful to explore during this conversation?

## The Conversation After the Conversation

○ Did I give the very best of myself to the Talent? If not, what can I do differently next time?

○ Did I walk away empty—say everything that needed to be said?

○ Am taking inordinate ownership for the successes and failures that actually belong to the Talent?

As coaches, our goal is to pay attention to that second conversation, not in retrospect, but in the moment the conversation takes place. It takes practice and focus, but the voice in your head contains important truths that need first to be acknowledged, and then addressed in the coaching conversation.

People instinctively know where there is a disparity between their external and internal conversations. Something doesn't feel right. There is an underlying dissonance between what we are thinking and what we are saying, and we no longer feel free to express ourselves. Often we want to have the internal conversation but don't know how to bridge the gap between the truth we know in our heads and the surface-level external conversation. We feel a distinct tension between these simultaneous conversations, and we respond by putting an invisible barrier between the other person and ourselves. It's as if we quietly slide a screen across our hearts, but not so quietly that the other person doesn't know. They do know. Our smiles and reassurances don't ring true. They sense our withdrawal from the conversation and are aware that we have become less forthcoming and straightforward with our observations. They know we are holding something back.

## HAVING THE CONVERSATION WITH THE RIGHT PERSON

No matter how carefully the coach delivers it, hearing the truth is not always easy for the Talent. As a result, the coaching conversation can quickly become uncomfortable. Think back to a time when someone said something to you that really put you over the edge and made you absolutely furious. You probably stomped out of a room, left a party early, or slammed a door. But was there some truth in what was said? Upon reflection, were you over-reacting because you did not want to be confronted with the issue? I have personally had coaching clients become so angry they have terminated the meeting, essentially kicking me out of the office or walking out themselves, only to return after a few minutes of reflection. As coaches, we need to learn to not take the Talent's anger personally, to persevere with our message to them, and to stick out these moments of discomfort.

When a conversation becomes uncomfortable, our most common reaction is to keep our truest thoughts and feelings to ourselves. Interestingly, we often feel perfectly comfortable having the conversation we should have had with the Talent with someone else instead. We use the third person as a conversational surrogate so that we do not have to endure the anxiety that comes with sharing difficult truths with the person to whom they should be directed. Behavioral psychologists call this process "triangulation." To the rest of us it is simply known as gossiping, complaining, or blaming.

It's understandable that we want to avoid conversations that we anticipate will be uncomfortable. But the master coach knows that the conversations need to happen anyway. He resolves to speak directly to the concerned party, and to no one else, about what is really on her mind. He eschews the water-cooler talk, in both her professional and personal life. The only time He talks about others in their absence is to honor them and their work.

## "YOU'RE BETTER THAN THIS"

As a young man, I loved to play hockey. I think there is something about the unrefined intensity of the sport that brought out my primal emotions and provided a temporary refuge from the modern world. Maybe I just liked being a warrior for a moment. During one hockey game, a coach for the other team said something to me that still rings in my ears. This was an especially rough game and I was deep into my primeval behavior (read: I was playing dirty). Late in the game, as I was skating past the opposition bench, I saw the coach leaning forward to give me a verbal blast. Hockey coaches are renowned for their ability to deliver a searing, expletive-laced communiqué in a matter of seconds so

I didn't think too much of it as I approached him. But this man's words were unexpected and haunt me to this day.

"Hey you, number seventeen," he shouted. "I've been watching you. You're better than this!" I was pierced to the core. He may as well have kicked my skates out from under me. At some level I already knew that my behavior was beneath me, and he had confronted me with what I already knew to be true. To this day, whenever I find myself opting for the lower road, his words ring crystal clear in my head. "You're better than this!" is the confrontation of the true coach.

## A LIGHTER TOUCH?

All this talk of confrontation may have you reaching for your megaphone. So let's pause for a moment. Confrontation doesn't always have to be dramatic. I learned this lesson one day early in my career as a coach. After a particularly difficult coaching session that was probably more emotionally charged than it needed to be, my client, leaning in for full effect, asked, "You are a bit of an in-your-face coach; are you this way with all your clients?" This gave me pause. Does confronting the Talent mean we need to be "in his face" all the time? I suggest not. Mariners know that most sailing requires the lightest of touches. Anything more causes the boat to swerve and lose momentum. Many times, the coach needs to use a light touch to help the Talent navigate through the waters of change. The Talent will rarely know how hard we are working to give them the freedom necessary for their great expectations to be realized!

Using a lighter touch means paying attention to what you want to do or say and asking yourself whether your words will be an improvement on silence. Does it need to be said? Does what you want to do need to be done? Or, would the Talent be best served if you did nothing? Sometimes doing nothing is the most difficult and profound thing we can do to assist another.

# DO IT ANYWAY

Even after many years of coaching senior executives, it's still not easy for me to confront people with the truth. Over time, however, I have learned to recognize when my internal voice is telling me something that I need to share. I do not particularly enjoy being confronted either. But if someone comes to me and says, "Gregg, this is difficult for me to tell you, but I think you need to know this," I find that I am open to the message and grateful to the messenger. Why? Because the messenger clearly has my interests at heart and cares enough about me to suffer some discomfort on my behalf. Most of us don't recognize our first moment of true confrontation because it doesn't feel the way we expect it to. In much the same way that courage is really about being terrified of something and doing it anyway, confrontation means being afraid of what your knowledge might mean for the Talent and telling them anyway, believing that no matter where the conversation leads, there will be good at the end of it.

However they feel in the moment, if you speak the truth, the Talent will probably remember your words and how the conversation made them feel for a long time. Simply put, when you confront with understanding and intention sourced in honesty and kindness, the Talent will respect and trust you, and your coaching will have a remarkable effect.

# THE COMPASSIONATE COACH

Having made this case for confrontation, I will close with a caveat: It's critical to know when to stop. Picture this: You are deep into a difficult, emotional conversation. The Talent is at the crossroads of potentially making a major change in their life. They are at a very difficult place—teetering on the edge. You desperately want to give them that one last shove to move them into a new possibility. Don't! It's their job to find the strength to take the step they know they needs to. Your job: just sit there. Be with them emotionally. Find a way to show that you understand and that you care. Lead with your compassion. That may be your most powerful intervention.

I believe that there are many styles of coaching that can be effective. I lean towards the challenging, confrontational end of the continuum. I believe that I can empathize with my clients and am sensitive to the difficulty in initiated real, sustained personal change. I also believe that my clients, who usually occupy very senior management roles in large corporations, function in a world replete with flattery, distortions, and misinformation, and that I can serve them best by helping them separate fact from fiction with regard to their personal leadership effectiveness. Usually, this involves a gut-wrenching process of feedback, assessment, reflection and facing up. But senior executives are human too. They fear, hurt and have self-doubts like the rest of us. I have learned one important thing: when someone is in the pit of despair as they are contemplating a major, personal change, the last thing they need is more challenging and confrontation. What they need is sincere compassion. And it is the coach's job to provide that, in the moment, in the coaching conversation.

# Top 10 Signs of Coaching Success

♦♦♦

*Good coaching doesn't always feel good. As a coach, it can be helpful to give the Talent some guidance as to the kinds of feelings they might encounter that indicate the coaching is working. I often share these top ten with my team and they share them widely with their clients.*

♦♦♦

*You know you are getting great coaching when . . .*

1. ***You are in the pit of despair.*** Many of your basic beliefs and assumptions about your role as a leader have been challenged, and you feel like you are losing your footing. You are seriously questioning your career to date and your personal aspirations.

2. ***You are really excited about the future.*** You don't know what the next chapter of your leadership career is going to look like, but you do know that there is no going back now. Something new and fresh awaits you.

3. ***You are angry, frustrated, and ready to fire your coach.*** None of your expectations for great pieces of advice and insights have been met. All you get are annoying questions like, "What will happen if your performance as a leader does not change?" and even more annoying statements such as, "I think you are much better than this."

4. ***You are feeling a little sheepish.*** Your coach has called you on the many ways you sell yourself short or get in your own way, and you have just realized you have been blaming others in the organization for holding you back when, in reality, most of your limitations have been self-imposed.

5. ***You have a renewed excitement about yourself as a leader.*** You have just realized that there is a huge gap between the leader you are and the leader you can be.

You've taken stock of your talents and strengths, and realized that you can have an enormous, lasting impact on your organization and the people in it. Very cool!

6. **You are shaken by some sharp, gut-wrenching feedback.** It's getting tougher to dismiss this feedback as the product of people who simply don't understand you or who have ulterior motives. What if this is actually true? What if I am wrong?

7. **You are feeling energized and powerful.** No longer a victim of organizational circumstances, you now have options and alternatives. You are committed to making your own choices and crafting your own leadership story. Wow!

8. **Your personal life has become brighter.** You now show up to your friends and family as a kind, caring and patient person who sees the very best in them and continually seeks out ways to serve them. You have realized that you can only be the best possible leader at work by being the best possible person at home.

9. **You have stopped wasting your precious time and energy.** You have embraced your emotions and become their master, not their slave. You have ceased to burn emotional energy reacting to organizational issues that you cannot influence and people you cannot control. You have developed an inner muscle that gives you the strength to choose your own best leadership actions and reactions.

10. **Remarkably . . . the people around you have changed for the better.** Somehow, the under-performers, sloths, and misfits that used to be ever-present are now gone and have been replaced with wonderfully creative and highly-engaged teammates. Interesting!

# 19

# Walk Away Empty

*Even if your hands are shakin'*
*And your faith is broken*
*Even as the eyes are closin'*
*Do it with a heart wide open*
*A wide heart*

—JOHN MAYER, *Say*

When the coaching conversation comes to an end, do you feel complete? Did you say everything that needed to be said? Did you feel good about the interaction? If so, why? If not, what was missing? Did you hold something back? Was there something else you wish you had said or done? Did you leave the interaction feeling unsettled, still filled with your real concerns and all the thoughts you censored, left to ruminate on them indefinitely? Or are you at peace, knowing that you gave it everything you could, in that moment?

The master coach walks away empty from every coaching conversation. She knows that she has said the one thing that most needed to be said, whether it was an uncomfortable truth, an unexpected insight, a word of encouragement, or a fresh perspective. There is nothing left unspoken, and no regrets. There is also no investment in the outcome—in being liked, being proven right, being admired, or being respected. A wise coach leaves every conversation with a sense of peace and well-earned emptiness. The burden she carried is transformed into a wonderful gift for another.

Even if the message was very difficult for the other person to hear, if it is delivered with the other person's interests at heart, the coach can take comfort in knowing that she lived up to her own calling. She did not hold back in her communication; she respected the Talent enough to tell them the truth. She cared enough about their success to take the risk and to be uncomfortable for their benefit. For a true coach, that is all she needs to know. Her work is done, at least in that moment, and she can walk away empty.

# APPENDIX I

# Getting the Most out of Leadership Coaching: A Guide for the Talent

While coaching is a highly effective way of accelerating your development as a leader, it also represents a significant investment of time and money. Here are fourteen ways to get the most out of your leadership coaching experience.

**1. Craft a bold new future.** Challenge yourself to move up to a whole new level as a leader. Don't waste this opportunity by settling for minor changes and fine-tuning. Spend time early in the coaching process crafting a picture of the most ambitious future possible for you as a leader. When this picture both excites you and scares you, you will know you have the right one. Expect great things from yourself and the process.

**2. Drive the process.** Unlike most other learning and development processes, you are responsible for setting your own learning objectives, crafting session agendas and structuring the coaching schedule. This is your show. Take charge. And be very, very selfish. For once, it really is all about you.

**3. Steel yourself for a rocky road.** If the changes you need to make to really lift your game as a leader were obvious and easy, you would have made them already. Prepare mentally for the rigorous tasks of self-assessment, learning and personal change. Think about what you are willing to learn, invest, risk and sacrifice to become a better leader. Recognize that leadership development is impossible without personal development.

**4. Seek out new sources of feedback.** Invite the perspectives of others, especially the stuff that is hard to hear. Pick six people who regularly see you in your role as a leader, tell them that you are involved in a leadership development process, and ask them how you can better use your leadership talents to have a larger influence on others.

**5. Prepare well for each session.** Before each coaching session spend 15 minutes in quiet private contemplation creating an agenda for the coaching dialogue. What are the most important leadership issues facing you at this moment? How have you fared since the last coaching session? How can you best use your time with your coach? Spend another 15 minutes quieting your mind from the frenetic pace of day-to-day organization life. Do what you need to do to get yourself ready to explore new territory, challenge your current thinking and experiment with new leadership practices.

**6. Be at your best.** Schedule your coaching sessions for times when you are rested; not at the end of the work day when you are drained, tired and out of gas. Coaching is often an intense, arduous process and will be most rewarding when you are at your physical and emotional best.

**7. Focus on outcomes.** Great leadership is measured by one thing: the impact that you have on others. It is not about being popular or easy going. Keep asking yourself one question: "What can I do to help others on my team or in my organization become more aligned, engaged, committed, productive and innovative?" You are the instrument of leadership but are measured by how others perform.

**8. Hold on to the important stuff.** Use the coaching process to get exceptional clarity on those principles and aspirations that are most important in your role as a leader. Resolve to hold on to these at all costs. Significant, sustained change can only happen when it is rooted in your closely-held personal values.

**9. Let go of the unimportant stuff.** Use the coaching process to identify the assumptions, behaviors and habits that no longer serve you well and are best left behind. Think about this process as aggressively pruning your approach to leadership so that you can blossom into a much stronger leader.

**10. Always move forward.** Leave every coaching session with at least one specific action that will advance your leadership in some way and commit to completing this action before the next session. This will include things such as experimenting with a new practice, having a difficult conversation, redesigning how you invest your time, restructuring your personal strategies or acquiring the resources you need to meet your goals. As the Spanish proverb says: "Habits are like cobwebs, and then they become cables."

**11. Reflect on and generalize your learning.** After each coaching session, take 15 minutes of private time to reflect on your progress, crystallize your new learning and insights, and determine how you can apply these to other areas of your work and leadership.

**12. Use your coach well.** Don't waste time trying to impress your coach. Your coach assumes that you are a very talented, committed leader with the potential to make a much bigger impact on your team and organization. Your coach is not your personal advisor, counselor or therapist. You will get few recommendations and answers. Your coach, however, has great faith in your ability to chart your own future as a leader and will challenge you, encourage you, confront you, affirm you and provoke you . . . always in service of your learning and development.

**13. Develop the habit of being direct and candid.** Use the coaching process to expand your ability to give feedback and constructively confront others. Start with your coach. Let your coach know what is working for you, what isn't and what you would like changed.

**14. Celebrate your performance breakthroughs.** While coaching is often an arduous process, it can also be a wonderful adventure replete with amazing insights and great personal victories. Take time at each session to talk about your wins, no matter how small, and revel in your progress. Enjoy the journey. It will likely be one of the most rewarding times of your career.

# Notes

1. Gary Hamel, "Bureaucracy Must Die," *Harvard Business Review*, November 4, 2013, https://hbr.org/2014/11/bureaucracy-must-die, accessed April 2016.
2. Global Tolerance: The Values Revolution, http://www.globaltolerance.com/wp-content/uploads/2015/01/GT-Values-Revolution-Report.pdf, accessed April 2016.
3. Gary Hamel, "Reinventing Management at the Mashup: Architecture and Ideology," http://www.garyhamel.com/blog/reinventing-management-mashup-architecture-ideology, accessed April 2016.
4. Gallup Report: "State of the Global Workplace" (2013), http://www.gallup.com/poll/165269/worldwide-employees-engaged-work.aspx, accessed May 2016.
5. The International Coaching Federation and the Human Capital Institute, "Building a Coaching Culture for Increased Employee Engagement," 2015, http://coachfederation.org/coachingculture, accessed April 2016.
6. Annie Dillard, *The Writing Life* (Harper Perennial, 2013) p. 32.
7. Daniel Kahneman, *Thinking Fast and Slow*, (Farrar, Straus and Giroux, 2013) p. 4.
8. Eric Schmidt, "Everybody Needs a Coach," CNN Money, http://money.cnn.com/video/fortune/2009/06/19/f_ba_schmidt_google.fortune/, accessed April 2016.
9. "Epistemology, Fourth Order Consciousness, and the Subject-Object Relationship," interview of Robert Kegan by Elizabeth Debold in *What Is Enlightenment?* Issue 22, Fall/Winter 2002, 149.
10. Robert Kegan and Lisa Laskow Lahey, *Immunity to Change* (Harvard Business Review Press 2009) p. 2.
11. Ibid, p. 63.
12. Ibid, p. 59.
13. Ibid, p. 58.
14. Charles Feltman and Sue Annis Hammond, *The Thin Book of Trust: An Essential Primer for Building Trust at Work* (Thin Book Publishing, 2008), Kindle Edition. loc 79–80.

15. Ibid, loc. 100–101.

16. David Brooks, *The Road to Character* (Random House, 2015) p. 263.

17. "Measuring the Return on Character", *Harvard Business Review*, April 2015 issue (pp.20–21) https://hbr.org/2015/04/measuring -the-return-on-character, accessed April 2016.

18. Ralph Waldo Emerson, *Self Reliance and Other Essays*, (Dover Publications, 1993), 23.

19. Richard Feynman, Caltech's 1974 Commencement Address, http://calteches.library.caltech.edu/51/2/CargoCult.htm, accessed April 2016.

20. Victor Frankl, *Man's Search for Meaning* (Touchstone, 1984) pp. 74–75.

21. Daniel J. Siegel, *Pocket Guide to Interpersonal Neurobiology: An Integrative Handbook of the Mind* (Norton Series on Interpersonal Neurobiology, 2012) Kindle Edition, loc. 3837.

22. Rosamunde Stone Zander and Benjamin Zander, *The Art of Possibility*, (Harvard Business School Press, 2000) p. 199.

23. Sakyong Mipham, *Turning the Mind Into an Ally* (Penguin, 2004) p. 130.

24. Dylan Thomas, Letter to Henry Treece.

25. Martin Luther King, Jr., Sermon: "A Tough Mind and a Tender Heart," The King Center Digital Archives, http://www.thekingcenter.org/archive/ document/tough-mind-and-tender-heart-1, accessed May 2016

26. Rabindranath Tagore, *Stray Birds* (Macmillan, 1921), p. 15.

27. Robert Greenleaf, *Servant Leadership* (Paulist Press, 2002), p. 27.

28. From an unpublished paper shared with the author.

29. Boyd Clark and Ron Crossland, *The Leader's Voice* (SelectBooks, 2002) pp. 14–15.

30. Daniel Goleman (1995/1996), *Emotional Intelligence: Why It Can Matter More Than IQ*, p. 285.

31. Daniel Shapiro, "Why Repressing Emotions Is Bad for Business," *Harvard Business Review*, November 2009

32. Center for Creative Leadership, 2003, http://www.ccl.org/leadership/ pdf/assessments/skills_intelligence.pdf, accessed April 2016.

33. Daniel Golemen, *Emotional Intelligence: Why It Can Matter More Than IQ* (Bantam, 2005), p. 90.

34. Ibid), p. ix.

35. Daniel Goleman, *Working with Emotional Intelligence*, (Bloomsbury Publishing PLC, 1998) p. 94.

36. Daniel Goleman, "What Makes a Leader?" *"Harvard Business Review,* January 2004, https://hbr.org/2004/01/what-makes-a-leader, accessed April 2016.

37. Brene Brown on Empathy, RSA Shorts, Dec. 10, 2013, https://www.youtube.com/watch?v=1Evwgu369Jw, accessed April 2016.

38. James O'Toole, *Creating the Good Life: Applying Aristotle's Wisdom to Find Meaning and Happiness* (Rodale Books: 2005) pp. 228–9.

39. Carl Rogers, *On Becoming a Person: A Therapist's View of Psychotherapy,* (London: Constable and Company Ltd., 1961), p. ix.

40. David L. Cooperrider and Suresh Srivastva, "Appreciative Inquiry in Organizational Life," Research in Organizational Change and Development, (1987, Vol.1), pp 129-169.

41. Ibid.

42. R. Rosenthal and L. Jacobson, Pygmalion in the Classroom, (New York: Rinehart and Winston, 1968).

43. Robert Tauber, Self-Fulfilling Prophecy: A Guide to Its Use in Education, (Westport, CT: Greenwood Publications, 1997).

44. NPR Morning Edition: "Teachers' Expectations Can Influence How Students Perform," September 17, 2012, http://www.npr.org/sections/health-shots/2012/09/18/161159263/teachers-expectations-can-influence-how-students-perform, accessed April 2016.

45. Susan Scott, *Fierce Conversations* (Berkley, 2004) pp. 222–228.

46. Daniel Kahneman, *Thinking Fast and Slow* (Farrar, Strauss & Giroux, 2011) p. 44.

47. Hansgrohe Report: "Shower for the Freshest Thinking," http://www1.hansgrohe.com/assets/at--de/1404_Hansgrohe_Select_ConsumerSurvey_EN.pdf, accessed April 2016.

48. Nick Stockton, "What's Up With That: Your Best Thinking Happens in the Shower" *Wired,* August 2014, http://www.wired.com/2014/08/shower-thoughts/, accessed April 2016.

49. Albert Einstein, Letter to Dr. H. L. Gordon (3 May 1949), as quoted in Walter Isaacson, *Einstein: His Life and Universe* (Simon & Schuster, 2011) p. 113.

50. Carl Jung, *Psychological Types*, (Princeton University Press, 1976) p. 367.

51. Malcolm Gladwell, *Blink: The Power of Thinking Without Thinking*, (New York: Little, Brown & Co., 2005), pp. 3–8.

Bluepoint Leadership Development is widely recognized as one of the finest coach-training companies in the world. We provide a complete suite of coaching programs and services that are designed to satisfy all of the coaching and performance development needs of any organization. Our core workshops include:

## LEADER AS COACH

The *Leader As Coach Workshop* is the gold standard in coach-training programs. Thousands of leaders at all levels of the organization have graduated from this two-day, highly experiential workshop with immediately usable coaching skills and approaches. Workshop participants learn how to apply the practices associated with the The 3C Model of Coaching and The 3 Coaching Power Tools in real-time coaching sessions.

This is an intense professional and personal development experience. Participants are challenged to become the kind of leaders who are welcomed into dynamic coaching relationships and conversations that result in sustained changes in performance, attitudes, and careers.

## THE COACHING ESSENTIALS

*The Coaching Essentials Workshop* is specifically designed for first-level supervisors, early-stage leaders, and individual contributors needing to build foundational coaching and interpersonal competencies. This one-day program equips participants with the necessary skills and tools to effectively initiate and conduct coaching conversations on topics such as performance improvement, talent development, and team effectiveness. This is a feedback-centered experience in which participants practice coaching in real-time conversations and receive direct advice and guidance on how they can increase their personal effectiveness in such conversations.

## ADVANCED COACHING SKILLS

This is a master's level, one-day workshop aimed at helping experienced coaches, seasoned leaders, and graduates of the *Leader As Coach Workshop* significantly enhance their coaching impact. Participants are guided through a profound learning journey in which they discover ways they can use their natural coaching talents to help others make significant changes in their approaches to work, careers, and life. During the course of the workshop, participants will learn the unique *Holding On—Letting Go—Moving On* coaching methodology, which is a disciplined, highly-personalized approach to performance improvement and career acceleration.

Virtual editions of all the above workshops are available.

For more information on these workshops, please visit us at www.bluepointleadership.com

# Index

# About the Author

Photograph by Brian Gottmers

**Gregg Thompson** is President of Bluepoint Leadership Development, recognized as one of the finest providers of coach-training programs in the world. Having coached many of the most senior leaders in Fortune 100 companies and trained thousands of coaches worldwide, Gregg is uniquely qualified to write the definitive book on what it takes to be a Master Coach. An in-demand speaker and facilitator, he has a broad-reaching background in leadership development, specifically in helping leaders develop their coaching skills. He has designed several award-winning leadership development workshops including The Coaching Essentials, Leader as Coach, Advanced Coaching Skills, and Powerful Coaching Conversations.

Gregg is the author of the popular book, *Unleashed!* (Select-Books, 2006). His deep corporate and consulting experience includes having held several senior executive roles in large commercial organizations, and his consulting, coaching, and training work has taken him to more than in forty-five countries. Gregg is a graduate of the British Columbia Institute of Technology (engineering technologist) and Pepperdine University (master of science in organization development). He writes several articles on coaching each year for industry publications, delivers multiple webinars and keynote speeches, and designs and facilitates custom coaching workshops. He is particularly well known for leading large group, highly interactive keynote coaching workshops for corporate meetings and conferences that provide participants with immediately usable coaching skills and approaches. Gregg can be reached at greggthompson@ bluepointleadership.com